THE TUDORS

THE TUDORS

•

John Guy

A BRIEF
INSIGHT

STERLING

New York / London
www.sterlingpublishing.com

STERLING and the distinctive Sterling logo are registered trademarks of
Sterling Publishing Co., Inc.

Library of Congress Cataloging-in-Publication Data Available

10 9 8 7 6 5 4 3 2 1

Published by Sterling Publishing Co., Inc.
387 Park Avenue South, New York, NY 10016

Published by arrangement with Oxford University Press, Inc.

First published in 1984 as chapter 5 in *The Oxford Illustrated History of Britain*,
the text of this book was revised and expanded in 2000.
Original text © Oxford University Press 1984; expanded and revised text © John Guy 2000.
Illustrated edition published in 2010 by Sterling Publishing Co., Inc.
Additional text © 2010 Sterling Publishing Co., Inc.

Distributed in Canada by Sterling Publishing
c/o Canadian Manda Group, 165 Dufferin Street
Toronto, Ontario, Canada M6K 3H6

Book design: The DesignWorks Group

Please see picture credits on page 158 for image copyright information.

Printed in China
All rights reserved

Sterling ISBN 978-1-4027-7539-0

For information about custom editions, special sales, premium and
corporate purchases, please contact Sterling Special Sales
Department at 800-805-5489 or specialsales@sterlingpublishing.com.

Frontispiece: This detail from *The Family of Henry VIII*, a c. 1545 royal portrait by an unknown
artist, shows young Prince Edward to the left of the king. To the right is Jane Seymour, his third wife.

CONTENTS

•

HONI SOIT QVI MALY PENCE

SEMPER · EADEM

SOIT QVI MAL

HONI SOIT PENCE

1 2 3 4 5 6 7 8 9 10

The Scale of English miles ✳ Roberto Adamo Authore 1588

NORTH

ONE

Economic Changes

•

THE AGE OF THE TUDORS has left its impact on the English-speaking world as a watershed. Hallowed tradition, native patriotism, and post-imperial gloom have united to swell our appreciation of the period as a golden age. Names alone evoke a phoenix-glow—Henry VIII, Elizabeth I, and Mary Stuart among the sovereigns of England and Scotland; Wolsey, William Cecil, and Leicester among the politicians; Marlowe, Shakespeare, Hilliard, and Byrd among the creative artists. The splendors of the court of Henry VIII; the fortitude of Sir Thomas More; the making of the English Bible, Prayer Book, and Church of England; the development of Parliament; the defeat of the Armada; the Shakespearian moment; and the legacy of Tudor domestic architecture—these are the undoubted climaxes of a simplified orthodoxy in which genius, romance, and tragedy are superabundant.

The insignia of the Order of the Garter—Britain's highest order of chivalry—are shown in this detail from an Elizabethan-era map.

Reality is inevitably more complex, less glamorous, and more interesting than myth. The most potent forces within Tudor England were often social, economic, and demographic ones. Thus if the period became a golden age, it was primarily because the considerable growth in population that occurred between 1500 and the death of Elizabeth I did not so dangerously exceed the capacity of available resources, particularly food supplies, as to precipitate a Malthusian crisis. Famine and disease unquestionably disrupted and disturbed the Tudor economy, but they did not raze it to its foundations, as in the fourteenth century. More positively, the increased manpower and demand that sprang from rising population stimulated economic growth and the commercialization of agriculture, encouraged trade and urban renewal, inspired a housing revolution,

Plague was a near-constant presence in late medieval Europe. This illustration of the *danse macabre*—from a c. 1526 series of woodcuts by Hans Holbein the Younger—presents a reminder that death will come to all, no matter their station.

enhanced the sophistication of manners, especially in London, and (more arguably) bolstered new and exciting attitudes among the English people, notably individualistic ones derived from Reformation ideals and Calvinist theology.

Recovery of Population

The matter is debatable, but there is much to be said for the view that England was economically healthier, more expansive, and more optimistic under the Tudors than at any time since the Roman occupation of Britain. Certainly, the contrast with the fifteenth century was dramatic. In the hundred or so years before Henry VII became king of England in 1485, England had been under-populated, under-developed, and inward-looking compared with other Western states, notably France. The country's recovery after the ravages of the Black Death had been slow—slower than in France, Germany, Switzerland, and some Italian cities. The process of economic recovery in preindustrial societies was basically one of recovery of population, and figures will be useful. On the eve of the Black Death (1348), the population of England and Wales was between 4 and 5 million; by 1377, successive plagues had reduced it to 2.5 million. Yet the figure for England (without Wales) was still no higher than 2.26 million in 1525, and it is transparently clear that the striking feature of English demographic history between the Black Death and the reign of Henry VIII is the stagnancy of population which persisted until the 1520s. However, the growth of population rapidly accelerated after 1525 (see page 4).

Between 1525 and 1541 the population grew extremely fast, an impressive burst of expansion after long inertia. This rate of growth

English Population Totals 1525–1601

YEAR	POPULATION TOTAL IN MILLIONS
1525	2.26
1541	2.77
1551	3.01
1561	2.98
1581	3.60
1601	4.10

Source: E. A. Wrigley and R. S. Schofield, *The Population History of England, 1541–1871*, London, 1981)

• • • • •

slackened off somewhat after 1541, but the Tudor population continued to increase steadily and inexorably, with a temporary reversal only in the late 1550s, to reach 4.1 million in 1601. In addition, the population of Wales grew from about 210,000 in 1500 to 380,000 by 1603.

Problems of Adjustment

While England reaped the fruits of the recovery of population in the sixteenth century, however, serious problems of adjustment were encountered. The impact of a sudden crescendo in demand, and pressure on available resources of food and clothing, within a society that was still overwhelmingly agrarian was to be as painful as it was, ultimately, beneficial. The morale of countless ordinary English people was to be wrecked by problems that were too massive to be ameliorated either by governments or by traditional, ecclesiastical philanthropy. Inflation, speculation in land, enclosures, unemployment, vagrancy, poverty, and urban squalor were the most pernicious evils of Tudor England, and these were the wider symptoms of population growth and agricultural commercialization. In the fifteenth century farm rents had been discounted, because tenants were so elusive; lords had abandoned direct exploitation of their demesnes, which were leased to tenants on favorable terms. Rents had been low, too, on peasants' customary holdings; labor services had been commuted, and servile villeinage had virtually disappeared by 1485. At the same time, money wages had risen to reflect the contraction of the wage-labor force after 1348, and food prices had fallen in reply to reduced market demand. But rising demand after 1500 burst the bubble of artificial prosperity born of stagnant population. Land hunger led to soaring rents. Tenants of farms and copyholders were evicted by business-minded landlords. Several adjacent farms would be conjoined, and amalgamated for profit, by outside investors at the expense of sitting tenants. Marginal land would be

Of the various types of husbandry, dairy farming was best suited to domestic producers. Although much milk had to be converted into butter or cheese before it could be sold, the necessary butter churns, cheese tubs, and other equipment were inexpensive. This woodcut of a woman churning butter is from *The Boke of Distyllacyon*, 1527.

converted to pasture for more profitable sheep-rearing. Commons were enclosed, and waste land reclaimed, by landlords or squatters, with consequent extinction of common grazing rights. The literary opinion that the active Tudor land market nurtured a new entrepreneurial class of greedy capitalists grinding the faces of the poor is an exaggeration. Yet it is fair to say that not all landowners, claimants, and squatters were scrupulous in their attitudes; a vigorous market arose among dealers in defective titles to land, with resulting harassment of many legitimate occupiers.

The greatest distress sprang, nevertheless, from inflation and unemployment. High agricultural prices gave farmers strong incentives to produce crops for sale in the dearest markets in nearby towns, rather than for the satisfaction of rural subsistence. Rising population, especially urban population, put intense strain on the markets themselves: demand for food often outstripped supply, notably in years of poor harvests due to epidemics or bad weather. In cash terms, agricultural prices began to rise faster than industrial prices from the beginning of the reign of Henry VIII, a rise which accelerated as the sixteenth century progressed. In real terms, the price rise was even more volatile than it appeared to be, since population growth ensured that labor was plentiful and cheap, and wages low. The size of the workforce increasingly exceeded available employment opportunities; average wages and living standards declined accordingly. Men (and women) were prepared to do a day's work for little more than board wages; able-bodied persons, many of whom were peasants displaced by rising rents or the enclosure of commons, drifted in waves to the towns in quest of work.

The best price index hitherto constructed covers the period 1264–1954, and its base period is most usefully 1451–75—the end of the fifteenth-century era of stable prices. From this index, we may follow the fortunes of wage-earning consumers, because the calculations are based on the fluctuating costs of composite units of the essential foodstuffs and manufactured goods, such as textiles, that made up an average family shopping basket in southern England at different times. Two indexes are, in fact, available: first the annual price index of the composite basket of consumables; secondly the index of the basket expressed as the equivalent of the annual wage rates of building craftsmen in southern England. No one supposes that building workers were typical of the labor force in the sixteenth century, or at any other time. But the indexes serve as a rough guide to the appalling reality of the rising household expenses of the majority of English people in the Tudor period:

Indexes (1451–75 = 100) of (1) price of composite unit of consumables; (2) equivalent of wage rate of building craftsman

YEAR	(1)	(2)
1450	102	98
1490	106	94
1510	103	97
1530	169	59
1550	262	48
1570	300	56
1590	396	51
1610	503	40

Source: E. H. Phelps Brown and S. V. Hopkins, *Economica*, no. 92, Nov. 1956, n.s. vol. xxiii)

It is clear that in the century after Henry VIII's accession, the average prices of essential consumables rose by some 488 percent. The price index stood at the 100 or so level until 1513, when it rose to 120. A gradual rise to 169 had occurred by 1530, and a further crescendo to 231 was attained by 1547, the year of Henry VIII's death. In 1555 the index reached 270; two years later, it hit a staggering peak of 409, though this was partly due to the delayed effects of the currency debasements practiced by Henry VIII and Edward VI. On the accession of Elizabeth I, in 1558, the index had recovered to a median of 230. It climbed again thereafter, though more steadily: 300 in 1570, 342 in 1580, and 396 in 1590. But the later 1590s witnessed exceptionally meager harvests, together with regional epidemics and famine: the index read 515 in 1595, 685 in 1598, and only settled back to 459 in 1600.

The index expressed as the equivalent of the building craftsman's wages gives an equally sober impression of the vicissitudes of Tudor domestic life. An abrupt decline in the purchasing power of wages occurred between 1510 and 1530, the commodity equivalent falling by some 40 percent in 20 years. The index fell again in the 1550s, but recovered in the next decade to a position equivalent to two-thirds of its value in 1510. Apart from 1586–87, it then remained more or less stable until the 1590s, when it collapsed to 39 in 1595, and to 29 in 1597. On the queen's death in 1603 it had recovered to a figure of 45—which meant that real wages had dropped by 57 percent since 1500.

Growth and Its Effects

When the percentage change of population in the sixteenth century is plotted against that of the index of purchasing power of a building

Percentage change of population since last total (Source: E. A. Wrigley and R.S. Scholfield, *The Population History of England, 1541-1871*, London, 1981)

– – – – Percentage change since last total (averaged over three years) in index of purchasing power of building craftsman's wages as compared to index of his purchasing power in 1510 (Source: E.H. Phelps Brown and S.V. Hopkins, *Economica*, no. 92, Nov. 1956, n.s. vol. xxiii)

• • • • •

craftsman's wages over the same period, it is immediately plain that the two lines of development are opposite and commensurate (see graph). Living standards declined as the population rose; recovery began as population growth abated and collapsed between 1556 and 1560. Standards then steadily dropped again, until previous proportions were overthrown by the disasters of 1586–87 and 1594–98—though the cumulative increase in the size of the wage-labor force since 1570 must also have had distorting effects.

In other words, population trends, rather than government policies, capitalist entrepreneurs, European imports of American silver, the more rapid circulation of money, or even currency debasements, were the key factor in determining the fortunes of the British Isles in the

Tudor farmers made use of varied plow designs depending on local soil conditions. The double-wheeled plow shown here was used on rocky soil, and was drawn by pairs of horses or oxen. This woodcut is from *The Boke of Husbandrie* (1523), an early English agriculture text.

sixteenth century. English government expenditure on warfare, heavy borrowing, and debasements unquestionably exacerbated inflation and unemployment. But the basic facts of Tudor economic life were linked to population growth.

In view of this fundamental truth, the greatest triumph of Tudor England was its ability to feed itself. A major national subsistence crisis was avoided. Malthus, who wrote his historic *Essay on the Principle of Population* in 1798, listed positive and preventive checks as the traditional means by which population was kept in balance with available resources of food. Preventive checks included declining fertility, contraception, and fewer, or later, marriages; positive ones involved heavy mortality and abrupt reversal of population growth. Fertility in England indeed declined in the later 1550s, and again between 1566 and 1571. In the reign of Elizabeth I, a higher proportion of the population than hitherto did not marry. Poor harvests resulted in localized starvation, and higher mortality, in 1481–83, 1519–21, 1527–29, 1544–45, 1549–51, 1554–56, 1586–87, and 1594–97, the most serious crop failures being in 1555–56 and 1596–97. In fact, as the effect of a bad harvest in any particular year lasted until the next good or average crop was gathered, the severest dearths lasted from 1555 to 1557, and from 1596 to 1598.

Yet devastating as dearth and disease proved for the affected areas, especially for the towns of the 1590s, the positive check of mass mortality on a national scale was absent even during the influenza epidemic of 1555–59. True, in addition to its other difficulties, Mary's regime faced the most serious mortality crisis since the Black Death: the population of England dropped by 200,000, or by 6 percent. But since some regions were relatively lightly affected, it is not proved that this was a national crisis in terms of its geographical extent. Population growth was only temporarily interrupted. Indeed, the chronology, intensity, and restricted geographical range of famine in the sixteenth century suggest that starvation crises in England were abating, rather than worsening, over time, while epidemics took fewer victims than before in proportion to the expansion of population. The countryside escaped crisis during two-thirds of Elizabeth's reign and the rural population remained in surplus. When the towns suffered an excess of deaths over births, this surplus was sufficient both to increase the numbers who stayed on the land and to compensate for urban losses by immigration to towns.

So there is much to be said for an optimistic view of the age of the Tudors. The sixteenth century saw the birth of Britain's preindustrial political economy—an evolving accommodation between population and resources, economics and politics, ambition and rationality. England abandoned the disaster-oriented framework of the Middle Ages for the new dawn of low-pressure equilibrium. Progress had its price, unalterably paid by the weak, invariably banked by the strong. Yet the tyranny of the price index was not ubiquitous. Wage rates for agricultural workers fell by less than for building workers, and some privileged groups of wage-earners such as the Mendip miners may have enjoyed a small rise in real income. Landowners, commercialized farmers, and property investors were the most obvious beneficiaries of a system that guaranteed fixed expenses and enhanced selling prices—it was in the Tudor period that the nobility, gentry, and mercantile classes alike came to appreciate fully the enduring qualities of land. The victims of Tudor economic changes were the poor. But many wage-laboring families were not wholly dependent upon their wages for subsistence. Multiple occupations, domestic self-employment, and cottage industries flourished, especially in the countryside; town-dwellers grew vegetables, kept animals, and brewed beer, except in the confines of London. Wage-laborers employed by great households received meat and drink in addition to cash income, although this customary practice was on the wane by the 1590s.

Anno H o s te octabz imago henrici vii taurus rege illustrissimi
ordinata u henrini zmil te regre

TWO

Henry VII

●

NO ONE NOW THINKS that the thirty years' civil commotion known as the Wars of the Roses amounted to more than an intermittent interruption of national life, or that Henry VII's victory at the battle of Bosworth Field (August 22, 1485) rates credit beyond that due to luck and good timing. Bosworth Field was, indeed, conclusive only because Richard III, together with so many of his household men and noble supporters, was slain in the battle; because Richard had eliminated in advance the most plausible alternatives to Henry VII; and because Henry was ingenious enough to proclaim himself king with effect from the day before the battle, thus enabling the Ricardian rump to be deemed traitors. By marrying Elizabeth of York, daughter of Edward IV, Henry VII then proffered the essential palliative to those Yorkist defectors who had joined

The first of the Tudor kings—Henry VII—is pictured here following a 1505 portrait by Michael Sittow. The red rose in the king's hand is a symbol of the House of Lancaster.

him against Richard in the first place. The ensuing births of Arthur in 1486, Margaret in 1489, Henry in 1491, and Mary in 1496 achieved the "Union of the Two Noble and Illustrious Families of Lancaster and York" upon which the pro-Tudor chronicler Edward Hall lavished the praise later echoed by Shakespeare's history plays.

The victor of Bosworth Field could found a new dynasty; it remained to be seen whether he could create a new monarchy. The essential demand was that someone should subordinate the nobility and position the English Crown above mere aristocratic faction. The king should not simply reign; he should also rule. For too long, the king of England had been "first among equals," rather than "king and emperor." The Wars of

The armies of Henry Tudor, Earl of Richmond (later, Henry VII), and Richard III meet on the battlefield at in 1485. Betrayed, the Yorkist king was unhorsed and went down amidst his enemies. This engraving from a nineteenth-century history book depicts Richard losing his crown.

the Roses had done negligible permanent damage to agriculture, trade, and industry, but they had undermined confidence in monarchy as an institution: the king was seen to be unable, or unwilling, to protect the rights of all his subjects. In particular, royal government had ceased to be politically neutral, having been excessively manipulated by individuals as an instrument of faction. All aspects of the system, especially the legal system, had been deeply permeated by family loyalties, aristocratic rivalries, favoritism, and a web of personal connections.

Refoundation of the Monarchy

In fairness to Edward IV, whom Sir Thomas More thought had left his realm "in quiet and prosperous estate," the work of refoundation had already been started. Edward IV's failure to make sufficient progress was primarily due to his excessive generosity, his divisive marriage to Elizabeth Woodville, and his barely controlled debauchery. His premature death had become the cue for the usurpation of Richard III, who was leader of a large and unusually powerful northern faction. Henry VII was, by contrast, dedicated and hardworking, astute and ascetic, and financially prudent to the point of avarice, or even rapacity, as some have maintained.

He cultivated a view of monarchy that was different to that of fifteenth-century England. His standpoint was modeled on the values of the new administrative monarchies of Europe, notably Brittany and France, where he had been in exile. He had no direct experience of government and administration before he became king. He was unconstrained by traditional values, and even risked destabilizing the monarchy by his bias against independent noble power. Fifteenth-century English rulers had been content to be the partners of the nobility. For Henry VII, in comparison, the goal was a monarchy in which the nobility served the king. To ensure the subordination of the nobles, he subverted their local and landed influence and took their gentry supporters into his own household. He had determined to rule England from his court and household, and not through the nobility. The risk was that if the nobles proved lukewarm at moments of crisis, Henry would be troubled by plots and rebellions for longer than he should have been.

Perkin Warbeck (c. 1474–99) lay claim to the throne by impersonating the younger son of Edward IV, Richard, Duke of York. Despite Warbeck's support from enemies of the Tudor monarch, Henry VII defeated the pretender's forces in Devonshire in 1497. Held in the Tower for treason, Warbeck was finally hanged in 1499. This sketch, for a portrait now lost, is by an unknown artist.

Of the two Yorkist impostures, that of Lambert Simnel as earl of Warwick in 1487, although the more exotic, was, thanks to Irish support, the more menacing; that of Perkin Warbeck, as Richard of York during the 1490s, was more easily contained despite Scottish involvement. Simnel was routed at Stoke (June 16, 1487); his promoters were killed or pardoned, and the young impostor was taken into the royal household as a servant. Warbeck fell into Henry's hands in August 1497; before long he had abused the king's leniency and was hanged in 1499. His demise was then made an occasion for executing the real earl of Warwick. But it was another seven years before the incarceration in the Tower of Edmund de la Pole, duke of Suffolk, completed the defensive process.

Conciliar Enforcement

Henry VII's mantra was enforcement—the enforcement of political and financial obligation to the Crown, as much as of law and order. In achieving the restoration of the monarchy, he held that ability, good service, and loyalty to the regime, irrespective of social origin and background, were to be the primary grounds of appointments, promotions, favors, and rewards. This belief was most evident in his use of royal patronage and in his appointments of councilors.

Patronage was the process by which the Crown awarded grants of offices, lands, pensions, annuities, or other valuable perquisites to its executives and dependants, and was thus its principal weapon of political control. Subjects, from great peers of the realm to humble knights and gentry, vied with each other for a share of the spoils—no noble was too high to join in the undignified scramble. Henry VII gradually restructured the patronage system to reflect more realistically the Crown's limited resources, and next ensured that the values of grants were fully justified in terms of return on expenditure. The resources of the monarchy were relatively meager in the years before the Dissolution of the Monasteries, and again in the later part of Elizabeth I's reign. Henry VII set the pace and the standards for distributing royal bounty for much of the sixteenth century; indeed, the only danger inherent in the Tudor model was that it might veer towards meanness or excessive stringency. The level and flow of grants might become so far diminished in relation to expectations as to foment impatience, low morale, and even active disloyalty among the Crown's servants and suitors.

Henry VII's councilors were all selected for their ability, assiduity, shrewdness, and loyalty. At first sight, Reynold Bray, Richard Empson, and Edmund Dudley seemed to hold quite minor offices.

Henry VII had "two instruments, Empson and Dudley (whom the people esteemed as his horse leeches and shearers) bold men and careless of fame, and that took toll of their master's grist. . . . These two persons being lawyers in science and privy councilors in authority, . . . turned law and justice into wormwood and rapine." —Francis Bacon, from *History of Henry VII* (1621) Henry VII conspires with his notorious councilors Richard Empson and Edmund Dudley in this imaginative nineteenth-century engraving.

Bray was chancellor of the duchy of Lancaster; soon after he died, in 1503, Empson succeeded him; Dudley was "president of the Council," which effectively meant minister without portfolio. But Bray and the rest exercised control, under the king, far in excess of their apparent status. For Henry VII managed in an absurdly short space of time to erect a network of financial and administrative checks and blueprints, the records of which never left the hands of himself and the selected few, and the methods of which were equally of their own devising. Financial accounting, the exploitation of the undervalued resources of the Crown lands along the most modern lines known to the land-holding aristocracy, the collection of fines and obligations, and the enforcement of Henry VII's morally dubious but probably necessary system of compelling political opponents, or even apparent friends, to enter into coercive bonds for good behavior—these vital matters were dealt with only by the king and his inner ring. It was a system that owed nothing to Parliament; it owed more to the Council in so far as Bray and the others sat there and spawned a new conciliar tribunal called the Council Learned in the Law; but it owed everything to the king himself, whose vigilance and attention to detail were invincible. Nothing slipped past Henry's keen eye. The extant Chamber books, the master-documents of the early Henrician nexus of conciliar enforcement, are signed, and thus checked, on every page, and even beside every entry, by the king, who was the best businessman ever to sit on the English throne.

Subordination of the Nobility

Henry VII's methods were a judicious combination of carrot and stick. In his large and active Council, he practiced consultation in a way that inspired, alternately, participation and boredom. All noblemen might be councilors before the reconstruction of the Council in the 1530s, and political identity depended on attending Council meetings from time to time. At Westminster the Council sat in Star Chamber (literally *camera stellata*, the room's azure ceiling being decorated with stars of gold leaf), which was both a meeting place for the working Council and a court of law. When Parliament was not in session, Star Chamber formed the chief point of contact between the Crown, its ministers, and the nobility until Wolsey's fall in 1529, and under Henry VII it discussed those issues, such as internal security, the armed defenses, and foreign affairs, which, of necessity, had to secure the support of the magnates, who were also the muster-men and captains of armies. The large Council never debated fiscal or enforcement policies under Henry VII, matters which remained firmly vested in the hands of ministers and those of the Council Learned in the Law and the Conciliar Court of Audit. But by making conciliar involvement a dimension of magnate status, Henry VII went far towards filtering out the threat of an alienated nobility that sprang from lack of communications and isolation in the political wilderness.

Next, Henry VII made a determined bid to concentrate the command of castles and garrisons, and, as far as possible, the supervision of military functions, in the hands of his courtiers, and he launched direct attacks on the local, territorial powers of the nobles, if he felt that those powers had been exercised in defiance of perceived royal interests. Such attacks normally took one of two forms, either that of prosecutions and fines at law for misfeasance, or the more drastic resort of attainder and forfeiture.

George Neville, Lord Abergavenny, for instance, was tried in King's Bench in 1507 on a charge of illegally retaining what amounted to a private army. He pleaded guilty (people did under Henry VII, for it was cheaper), and was fined £70,650*, being the price, at the rate of £5 per man per month, for which he was liable for having hired 471 men for 30 months from June 10, 1504 to December 9, 1506. It seems that the "army" comprised 25 gentlemen, 4 clerics, 440 yeomen, 1 cobbler, and 1 tinker—the Tudors got details right. But Henry VII was not opposing retaining on principle on the occasion of this prosecution; he *valued* Abergavenny's force, down to that last Kentish tinker, just as much as did its true territorial proprietor—it was even better that Abergavenny was footing the bill. Despite Henry VII's peaceful foreign policy, he brought

---

*Monetary figures are in British pounds throughout, as conversion to modern figures and other currencies is less meaningful than the relative amounts. Suffice to say that £5 per month was a substantial figure, and the fine was comparable to millions of modern dollars.

England into the mainstream of European affairs, quite apart from her fluctuating relations with Scotland. The all-too-brief marriage of Prince Arthur to Catherine of Aragon in 1501 considerably raised Henry VII's prestige in Europe, while his treaty with Anne of Brittany obliged him briefly to invade France in 1492. England, or rather the king of England, had virtually no army beyond that recruited on demand from the royal demesne, and that provided on request by the nobility. Thus, in Abergavenny's case, which was exemplary and admonitory, it was especially relevant that the accused was by birth a Yorkist, and that he had been implicated in an unsuccessful rising of Cornishmen in 1497.

Far more drastic was the weapon of attainder and forfeiture. Acts of attainder were parliamentary statutes proclaiming convictions for treason, and declaring the victim's property forfeit to the king and his blood "corrupted." The method almost always involved execution of the victim, but did not necessarily lead to the total forfeiture of his lands. Most attainders were by tradition repealed later in favor of the heirs, though not always with full restoration of property. Henry VII's reign saw 138 persons attainted, and 86 of these attainders were never reversed. Only 46 were reversed by Henry VII, and 6 by Henry VIII. These figures compare unfavorably with those of the reigns of Henry VI, Edward IV, and even Richard III—reflecting the toughness of Tudor policy. Henry VII realized that attainders were not simply a tool of faction and dynastic intrigue: they could be used to subdue "overmighty" or hostile magnates, while at the same time significantly augmenting the Crown's own power and income. In similar fashion, Henry VIII, after the Pilgrimage of Grace (1536), and Elizabeth I, after the Northern Rising (1569), used attainders to bolster the Crown's territorial strength and eradicate magnate resistance. Finesse was required if the method was not to backfire. Its excessive use,

The popular uprising known as Ket's Rebellion began on Mousehold Heath, near Norwich in Norfolk. Robert Ket was a tanner and lesser landowner who led a mass protest that turned into a revolt against the crown in 1549. Ket was said to have dispensed justice beneath a tree, which came to be called the "Oak of Reformation." The rebels' demands included an end to enclosures and other appropriations of the commons for private use by the wealthy.

and repeated failure to reverse attainders in favor of heirs, could spark resentment among the peerage. Attainders could also do serious damage if they left a power vacuum in a particular region, as occurred in East Anglia when the third duke of Norfolk was attainted by Henry VIII in 1547. His attainder, reversed by Mary in 1553, created instability which the Crown could not easily correct, and paved the way for Ket's Rebellion in 1549.

"Financial Rapacity"

Historians suspect that Henry VII overdid his policy of enforcement in the latter part of his reign. In 1506, he commissioned one Polydore Vergil, who was a visiting collector of papal taxes, to write a history of England, and it was Polydore who claimed that the first of the Tudors had practiced financial rapacity after 1502:

For he began to treat his people with more harshness and severity than had been his custom, in order (as he himself asserted) to ensure that they remained more thoroughly and entirely in obedience to him. The people themselves had another explanation for his action, for they considered they were suffering not on account of their own sins but on account of the greed of their monarch. It is not indeed clear whether at the start it was greed; but afterwards greed did become apparent.

The debate concerning the king's methods and intentions still rages. Whatever the eventual outcome, three points are proven. First, Henry VII used penal bonds in sums ranging from £100 to £10,000 to enforce what *he* considered to be acceptable behavior on his subjects. These bonds aimed to hold the political nation, especially the nobility, at the king's mercy, and to short-circuit due process of common law in case of offense by the victims. If anyone was deemed to have misbehaved, he would simply be sued for debt on his bond—it was not possible to litigate over the nature or extent of the alleged offense. In other words, Henry VII used bonds to defeat the law in the way that King John and Richard II had used blank charters. Second, Empson and Dudley corrupted juries to find verdicts in favor of Henry VII's feudal rights. The best example is the case of the estates of the earl of Westmorland. A conciliar inquiry had to be launched to rectify this matter in Henry VIII's reign. Lastly, Henry VII sold offices, including legal ones. He twice sold the chief justiceship of the Court of Common Pleas, and at high prices. He also sold the posts of attorney-general, Master of the Rolls, and Speaker of the House of Commons.

It has long been a platitude that Henry VII restored stability after the Wars of the Roses. As Francis Bacon maintained, there was now "no such thing as any great or mighty subject who might eclipse or overshadow the imperial power." The first of the Tudors enhanced the prestige of the monarchy, its financial resources, and its regional authority. He turned his court into the crucible of politics and the magnates into a service nobility. Above all, he perpetuated his dynasty by ensuring the succession of his surviving son, Henry VIII. On the other hand, his fiscal success has been vastly overrated. It is unlikely that he left a vast treasure, as Bacon later claimed. Regular Crown income was £113,000 per annum by the end of the reign, but had risen as high as £120,000 under Richard III and £160,000 under Edward III. Again, Henry VII's England was something of a bureaucrat's paradise. The king was too mean to pay his administrators properly: a culture of acquisitiveness permeated his administration. His councilors were capable of penalizing landowners on their own account, and of fixing their own deals in order to build landed fortunes for themselves. Apart from Bray, the classic instance is Sir Henry Wyatt, who purchased land at knock-down prices from people who were unable to pay their debts to the Crown. Did the king know that they were doing this, pretending otherwise in order to be able to attaint them if they put a foot wrong, or was he less competent than he has always seemed?

Finally, Henry VII passed on his throne to his son, but not automatically. His innermost courtiers sought primarily to ensure their own survival. Henry died at 11 p.m. on April 21, 1509, but his death was kept secret until the afternoon of the 23rd, when it was announced to the main body of councilors and Henry VIII's accession was proclaimed. The delay gave those at the seat of power time to protect themselves. A general pardon was issued that included treasons and felonies committed in Henry VII's reign, and Empson and Dudley, the two most hated councilors, were arrested. They were imprisoned in the Tower for a year, and

The Henry VII Chapel—depicted here in an eighteenth-century painting by Canaletto—was added to Westminster Abbey between the years 1503 and 1512, and remains a fine example of the Perpendicular Gothic style. King Henry VII was buried in the chapel upon his death in 1509.

then executed. This was a ploy to win popularity, and provide a scapegoat for the methods of the reign. Furthermore, Henry VII's executors, who were his innermost councilors, contrived that Henry VIII was not allowed fully to be king or to enjoy untrammeled sovereignty until Wolsey liberated him from these constraints. Henry VIII was not even allowed to sign his name to royal gifts or letters patent without the counter-signature of his father's "minders." If anything, the reign of Henry VII marked as much the triumph of the king's courtiers in politics as of the king himself.

· ETATIS ·   · SVÆ · XL

THREE

Henry VIII

●

HENRY VIII SUCCEEDED at barely eighteen years of age, because his elder brother, Arthur, had died in 1502. Under pressure from his father's executors, Henry began his "triumphant" reign by marrying his late brother's widow, Catherine of Aragon—a union that was to have momentous, not to say revolutionary, consequences. He continued by executing Empson and Dudley. His character was fascinating, threatening, and sometimes morbid. His egoism, self-righteousness, and capacity to brood sprang from the fusion of an able but second-rate mind with what looks suspiciously like an inferiority complex. Henry VII had restored stability and royal authority, but it may have been for reasons of character, as much as policy, that his son resolved to augment his regal power.

This portrait of Henry VIII in his prime (c. 1537–1542) was painted by an unknown artist in the studio of German Renaissance artist Hans Holbein the Younger.

It is likely that this image of a young woman wearing a necklace adorned with letter K is a portrait of Catherine of Aragon after her arrival in England from Spain when she was almost 16. Widowed at a young age, she subsequently wed her late husband's brother, King Henry VIII. Despite at least seven pregnancies, she would ultimately fail to produce a male heir, leading to the king's petition for an annulment.

As his reign unfolded Henry VIII added "imperial" concepts of kingship to existing "feudal" ones; he sought to give the words "king and emperor" a meaning unseen since the days of the Roman Empire. He was eager, too, to conquer—to emulate the glorious victories of the Black Prince and Henry V, to quest after the golden fleece that was the French Crown. He wished, in fact, to revive the Hundred Years War, despite the success of Valois France in consolidating its territory and the shift of emphasis of European politics towards Italy and Spain. Repeatedly the efforts of his more constructive councilors were bedeviled, and overthrown, by his chivalric dreams, and by costly wars that wasted men, money, and equipment. If, however, humanist criticism of warfare by Colet, Erasmus, and Thomas More is well known, it should not be forgotten that "honor" in the Renaissance was defended in the last resort by battle. "Honor" was the cornerstone of aristocratic culture; sovereign rulers argued that unlike their subjects they lacked "superiors" from whom redress of grievances might be sought, and so had no choice but to accept the "arbitrament" of war when diplomacy failed. Also, war was the "sport of kings." By competing dynastically and territorially with his European counterparts, especially Francis I, Henry

VIII acknowledged settled convention and, even more obviously, popular demand. His reign saw the boldest and most extensive invasions of France since the reign of Henry V. In fact, only a minority of contemporaries had any sense of the serious long-term economic damage that Renaissance warfare could inflict.

Evaluation is always a matter of emphasis, but on the twin issues of monarchic theory and lust for conquest, there is everything to be said for the view that Henry VIII's policy was consistent throughout his reign; that Henry was himself directing that policy; and that his ministers and officials were allowed freedom of action only within accepted limits, and when the king was too busy to take a personal interest in state affairs.

Wolsey and the Church

Cardinal Wolsey was Henry VIII's first minister, and the fourteen years of that proud but efficient prelate's ascendancy (1515–29) saw the king in a comparatively restrained mood. Henry, unlike his father, found writing "both tedious and painful"; he preferred hunting, dancing, dallying, and playing the lute. In his more civilized moments, Henry studied theology and astronomy; he would wake up Sir Thomas More in the middle of the night in order that they might gaze at the stars from the

The son of a butcher, Cardinal Thomas Wolsey rose to greatness as Lord Chancellor to Henry VIII. He fell from favor when he failed to obtain the annulment of the king's marriage to Catherine of Aragon, and died on his way to imprisonment in the Tower of London.

roof of a royal palace. He wrote songs, and the words of one form an epitome of Henry's youthful sentiments:

> Pastime with good company
> I love and shall until I die.
> Grudge who lust, but none deny;
> So God be pleased, thus live will I;
> For my pastance,
> Hunt, sing and dance;
> My heart is set
> All goodly sport
> For my comfort:
> Who shall me let?

Yet Henry himself set the tempo; his pastimes were only pursued while he was satisfied with Wolsey. Appointed lord chancellor and chief councilor on Christmas Eve 1515, Wolsey used the Council and Star Chamber as instruments of ministerial power in much the way that Henry VII had used them as vehicles of royal power—though Wolsey pursued uniform and equitable ideals of justice in Star Chamber in place of Henry VII's selective justice linked to fiscal advantage. But Wolsey's greatest asset was the unique position he obtained with regard to the English Church. Between them, Henry and Wolsey bludgeoned the pope into granting Wolsey the rank of legate *a latere* for life, which meant that he became the superior ecclesiastical authority in England, and could convoke legatine synods. Using these powers, Wolsey contrived to subject the entire English Church and clergy to a massive dose of Tudor government and taxation, and it looks as if an uneasy compromise prevailed behind the scenes in which Henry agreed that the Church was, for the moment, best controlled by a churchman who was a royal servant, and the clergy accepted that it was better to be obedient to an ecclesiastical rather than a secular tyrant—for it is unquestionably true that Wolsey protected the Church from the worst excesses of lay opinion while in office.

The trouble was that, with stability restored, and the Tudor dynasty apparently secure, England had started to become vulnerable to a mounting release of forces. It used to be argued that anti-clericalism was a major cause of the English Reformation, but this interpretation has lately been challenged. Recent research has established that the majority of late medieval English clergy were not negligent or unqualified: Church courts were not usually unfair; probate, mortuary, and tithes disputes were few; pluralism, absenteeism, nepotism, sexual misconduct, and commercial "moonlighting" by clergy were less serious than once was thought. On the other hand, there *were* priests who failed to hold services at the proper times, who did not preach, and whose habits were aggressive—the rector of Addington in Northamptonshire, cited before the Lincoln consistory court in 1526, had two children by his cook and marched about the village in chain-mail. In fact, it was all too easy for a priest to behave like other villagers: to make a mistress of his housekeeper, and to spend the day cultivating his glebe. Although the English Church was free of major scandals, such abuses as non-residence, pluralism, concubinage, and the parochial clergy's neglect to repair chancels, where these occurred, continued to attract attention. Also tithes disputes, probate and mortuary fees, charges for saying mass on special occasions, and the trial and burning of heretics could become flashpoints. In particular, it was pointed out by prominent writers, notably the grave and learned Christopher St. German (1460–1541), that the Church's procedure in cases of suspected heresy permitted secret accusations and hearsay evidence, and denied accused persons the benefit of purgation by oath-helpers or trial by jury, which was a Roman procedure contrary to the principles of English common law—a clerical plot to deprive the English of their natural, legal rights. Such ideas were manifestly explosive; for they incited division between clergy and common lawyers.

Late medieval religion was also sacramental and institutional. As the expectations of the educated laity mirrored those of the Renaissance, many people sought to found their faith on texts of Scripture and Bible stories (preferably illustrated ones), but vernacular Bibles were illegal in England—the Church authorities believed that the availability of an English Bible, even an authorized version, would foment heresy by permitting people to form their own opinions. Sir Thomas More, Wolsey's successor as lord chancellor, declared in his proclamation of June 22, 1530 that "it is not necessary the said Scripture to be in the English tongue and in the hands of the common people, but that the distribution of the said Scripture, and the permitting or denying thereof, dependeth only upon the discretion of the superiors, as they shall think it convenient." More pursued a policy of strict censorship: no books in English printed outside the realm on any subject whatsoever were to be imported; he forbade the printing of scriptural or religious books in England, too, unless approved in advance by a bishop. But More and the bishops were swimming against the tide. The invention of printing had revolutionized the transmission of new ideas across Western Europe, including Protestant ideas. Heretical books and Bibles poured from the presses of English exiles abroad, notably that of William Tyndale at Antwerp. The demand for vernacular Scriptures was persistent, insistent, and widespread; Henry VIII was enlightened enough to wish to assent to it, and publication of an official English Bible in Miles Coverdale's translation was first achieved in 1535, the year of More's execution.

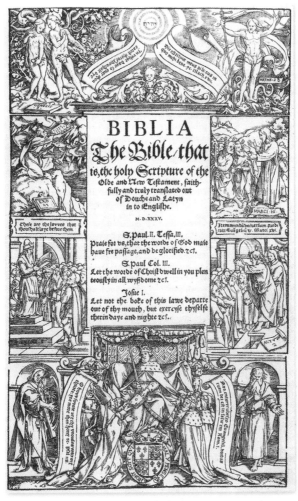

Holbein provided the engraving for the title page of the first printed English Bible (1535), known for its translator as the Coverdale Bible. The foot of the page shows Henry VIII enthroned as an "imperial" king. He hands the Bible to his bishops, flanked by King David playing the lyre and by St. Paul. David was a model for the royal supremacy, and St. Paul was revered as a symbol of evangelical freedom in contrast to the papacy.

Humanism and Lutheranism

Of the forces springing from the European Renaissance, humanism and the influence of classical learning came first. The humanists, of whom the greatest was Erasmus of Rotterdam (1467–1536), rejected scholasticism in favor of simple biblical piety, or *philosophia Christi*, which was founded on primary textual scholarship, and in particular study of the Greek New Testament. Erasmus made several visits to England, and it was in Cambridge in 1511–14 that he worked upon the Greek text of his edition of the New Testament.

The humanists first challenged the English establishment in 1511—when, preaching before Convocation, John Colet attacked clerical abuses and demanded reform of the Church from within. His sermon caused resentment, but the humanists continued to call for spiritual renewal. Erasmus embellished Colet's evangelism with racy criticisms of priests and monks, Catholic superstition, and even the papacy. He published his *Handbook of a Christian Knight* (1503), *Praise of Folly* (1511), and *Education of a Christian Prince* (1516) before Luther challenged the papacy. Also in 1516 he published his

This detail from a larger work by Lucas Cranach the Younger shows the circle of reformers with Martin Luther: (from right) Philipp Melanchthon, Caspar Cruciger, Justus Jonas, Erasmus of Rotterdam, Johannes Bugenhagen, Luther, Georg Spalatin, and Johannes Forster.

VTOPIAE INSVLAE FIGVRA

An illustration of the imaginary land Utopia from the first edition of More's work by the same name, first published in Latin in 1516.

Greek New Testament together with a revised Latin translation. Scholars and educated laity were delighted; at last they drank the pure waters of the fountainhead.

More's *Utopia* (1516) was more complex. It wittily idealized an imaginary society of pagans living on a remote island in accordance with principles of natural virtue. The Utopians possessed reason but lacked Christian revelation, and by implicitly comparing their benign social customs and enlightened attitudes with the inferior standards, in practice, of Christian Europeans, More produced an indictment of the latter based largely on deafening silence. For the irony and scandal was that Christians had so much to learn from heathens.

Yet the humanism of Colet, Erasmus, and More was fragile. Even without Luther's challenge it would have become fragmented because faith and reason in its scheme were at odds. More's solution was to argue that faith was the superior power and that Catholic beliefs must be defended because God commanded them, but Erasmus trusted human rationality and could not accept that God tested people's faith by making them believe things that Renaissance scholarship had thrown into question. Even Luther regarded Erasmus as an enemy because of his emphasis on reason. So these fissures weakened humanism and new exponents of reform caught public attention. In England, the influence of Lutheranism exceeded the small number of converts: the rise of the "new learning," as it was called, became the most potent of the forces released in the 1520s and 1530s.

Luther's ideas and numerous books rapidly penetrated the universities, especially Cambridge, the City of London, the inns of court, and even reached Henry VIII's court through the intervention of Anne Boleyn and her circle. At Cambridge, the young scholars influenced included Thomas Cranmer and Matthew Parker, both of whom later became archbishops of Canterbury. Wolsey belatedly made resolute efforts as legate to stamp out the spread of Protestantism, but without obvious success. His critics blamed his reluctance to burn men for heresy—for Wolsey would burn books and imprison men, but shared the humane horror of Erasmus at the thought of himself committing bodies to the flames. However, the true reason for Luther's appeal was that he had given coherent doctrinal expression to the religious subjectivity of individuals, and to their distrust of clerical power and papal monarchy. His view of the ministry mirrored the instincts of the laity, and his answer to concubinage was the global solution of clerical marriage.

The First Divorce

Into this religious maelstrom dropped Henry VIII's first divorce. Although Catherine of Aragon had borne five children, only the Princess Mary (b. 1516) had survived, and the king demanded the security of a male heir to protect the fortunes of the Tudor dynasty. It was clear by

Anne Boleyn became the second wife of Henry VIII in 1533, precipitating the break with Rome. Later the same year she gave birth to the princess Elizabeth, later to become Queen Elizabeth I. Accused of incest, adultery, and treason, she was tried, convicted, and beheaded with a sword in 1536. This portrait by an unknown artist is from Hever Castle in Kent, the home of the Boleyn family.

1527 that Catherine was past the age of childbearing; meanwhile Henry coveted Anne Boleyn, who would not comply without the assurance of marriage. Yet royal annulments were not infrequent, and all might have been resolved without drama, or even unremarked, had not Henry VIII been a proficient, if mendacious, theologian.

The chief obstacle was that Henry, who feared international humiliation, insisted that his divorce should be granted by a competent authority in England—this way he could deprive his wife of her legal rights, and bully his episcopal judges. But his marriage had been founded on Pope Julius II's dispensation, originally obtained by Henry VII to enable the young Henry VIII to marry his brother's widow, and hence the matter pertained to Rome. In order to have his case decided without reference to Rome, in face of the papacy's unwillingness to concede the matter, Henry had to prove against the reigning pope, Clement VII, that his predecessor's dispensation was invalid—then the marriage would automatically terminate, on the grounds that it had never legally existed. Henry would be a bachelor again. However, this strategy took the king away from matrimonial law into the quite remote and hypersensitive realm of papal power. If Julius II's dispensation was invalid, it must be because the successors of St. Peter had no power to devise such instruments, and the popes were thus no better than other human legislators who had exceeded their authority.

Henry was a good enough theologian to know that there was a minority opinion in Western Christendom to precisely this effect. He was enough of an egoist, too, to fall captive to his own powers of persuasion— soon he believed that papal primacy was unquestionably a sham, a ploy of human invention to deprive kings and emperors of their legitimate inheritances. Henry looked back to the golden days of the British imperial past, to the time of the Emperor Constantine and of King Lucius I. In fact, Lucius I had never existed—he was a myth, a figment of pre-Conquest imagination. But Henry's British "sources" showed that this Lucius was a great ruler, the first Christian king of Britain, who had endowed the British Church with all its liberties and possessions and then written to Pope Eleutherius asking him to transmit the Roman laws. However, the pope's reply explained that Lucius did not need any Roman law, because he already had the *lex Britanniae* (whatever that was) under which he ruled both Church and State:

> For you be God's vicar in your kingdom, as the psalmist says, "Give the king thy judgments, O God, and thy righteousness to the king's son" (Ps. lxxii: i) . . . A King hath his name of ruling, and not of having a realm. You shall be a king, while you rule well; but if you do otherwise, the name of a king shall not remain with you . . . God grant you so to rule the realm of Britain, that you may reign with him for ever, whose vicar you be in the realm.

Vicarius Dei—vicar of Christ. Henry's divorce had led him, incredibly, to believe in his royal supremacy over the English Church.

The Reformation and Cromwell

With the advent of the divorce crisis, Henry took personal charge of his policy and government. He ousted Wolsey, who was hopelessly compromised in the new scheme of things, since his legatine power came directly from Rome. He named Sir Thomas More to the chancellorship, but this move backfired owing to More's scrupulous reluctance to involve himself in Henry's proceedings. He summoned Parliament, which for the first time in English history worked with the king as an omnicompetent legislative assembly, if hesitatingly so. Henry and Parliament finally threw off England's allegiance to Rome in an unsurpassed burst of revolutionary statute-making: the Act of Annates (1532), the Act of Appeals (1533), the First Act of Succession (1534), the Act of Supremacy (1534), the Treasons Act (1534), and the Act against the Pope's Authority (1536). The Act of Appeals proclaimed Henry VIII's new imperial status—all English jurisdiction, both secular and religious, now sprang from the king—and abolished the pope's right to decide English ecclesiastical cases. The Act of Supremacy declared that the king of England was supreme head of the Church of England—not the pope. The Act of Succession was the first of a series of Tudor instruments used to settle the order of succession to the throne, a measure which even Thomas More agreed was in itself sound, save that this statute was prefaced by a preamble denouncing papal jurisdiction as a "usurpation" of Henry's imperial power. More, together with Bishop Fisher of Rochester, and the London Carthusians, the most ascetic and honorable custodians of papal primacy and the legitimacy of the Aragonese marriage, were tried for "denying" Henry's supremacy under the terms of the Treasons Act. These terms made it high treason maliciously to deprive either king or queen of "the dignity, title, or name of their royal estates"—that is, to deny Henry's royal supremacy. The victims of the act, who were in reality martyrs to Henry's vindictiveness, were cruelly executed in the summer of 1535. A year later the Reformation legislation was completed by the Act against the Pope's Authority, which removed the last vestiges of papal power in England, including the pope's "pastoral" right as a teacher to decide disputed points of Scripture.

Henry VIII now controlled the English Church as its supreme head. Yet why did bishops who held crucial votes in the House of Lords and Convocation permit the Henrician Reformation to occur? The answer

Pope Clement is suppressed under the feet of King Henry VIII in this sixteenth-century engraving symbolizing the king's seizure of spiritual authority as head of the Church of England.

is partly that Henry coerced his clerical opponents into submission by threats and punitive taxation; but some bishops actually supported the king, albeit reluctantly. They preferred to be ruled by the Tudors personally, with whom they could bargain and haggle, than be subordinated to Parliament, which was the alternative. As early as 1532 Cromwell had sought to make the Tudor supremacy parliamentary. But Parliament's contribution was cut back to the mechanical, though still revolutionary, task of enacting the requisite legislation. In Henry's view, the models for statecraft were the kings of Israel, especially David and Solomon, and the late Roman emperors, especially Constantine and Justinian, who governed both Church and State. Henry held his supremacy to be "imperial" despite the use of Parliament. Royal supremacy was "ordained by God"; all Parliament had done was belatedly to recognize the fact. Also it was not until 1549, 1552, and 1559 that the full implications of the break with

Rome became clear, when the royal supremacy became a Trojan horse for Protestantism. Not everyone realized what was happening in the 1530s. Many saw the Acts of Appeals and Supremacy as a temporary squabble between king and pope, a cause unworthy of martyrdom.

Before 1529 Henry had ruled his clergy through Wolsey; after 1534 he did so personally, and through his second minister, Thomas Cromwell. A former aide of Wolsey, Cromwell had risen to power as a client of the Boleyn interest. By January 1532 he had taken command of the machinery of government, especially the management of Parliament. And by exploiting the offices of Master of the Jewels, King's Secretary, Lord Privy Seal, and Henry's (lay) vicegerent in spirituals, he became chief policymaker under Henry until he fell in June 1540. This is significant, because historians increasingly think that Henry VIII and Cromwell had different "slants" on the Reformation. Whereas the king was a doctrinal conservative with largely orthodox views on the sacraments, Cromwell was a supporter of the evangelical Reformation. Thus Henry was not opposed on principle to the monastic ideal: he simply regarded the religious houses after the break with Rome as bastions of "popery" and of opposition to his second marriage. By contrast, Cromwell was anti-monastic: as vicegerent he sought the suppression of the monasteries as well as the

SIR THOMAS CROMWELL KNIGHT etc.

A staunch advocate of the English Reformation and a chief minister to Henry VIII, Thomas Cromwell was executed for heresy and treason in 1540.

abolition of shrines, the veneration of saints and images, pilgrimages, and the doctrine of purgatory, all on grounds of superstition.

The views of Henry VIII and Cromwell closely converged in respect of their desire to propagate the Bible in English among the people. But their reasons were different. Henry VIII interpreted the Bible as God's "efficacious Word"—almost a sacrament in itself, one which he personally distributed as supreme head of the Church, and which was not dependent upon the mediating role of the clergy. Overall, Henry imagined a "Church of England" which would retain Catholic doctrine, but curtail the influence of the clergy. This is why he was opposed to cults of saints, intercessions, and the use of images and pilgrimages for the people at large, but did not eradicate these traditional rites and ceremonies from the Chapel Royal. Cromwell was likewise a leading patron of the English Bible, but his position was completely different. He agreed with the Protestant reformers that Scripture was the supreme authority against which the Church and clergy should be judged. He sought the reform of the Church on biblical lines, in particular the extirpation of idolatry and unnecessary ceremonies. He did not deny the real presence of Christ in the Eucharist, nor did he teach the Lutheran doctrine of "justification by faith alone." But his emphasis on faith, the Bible, and the role of preaching put him in the reformed camp. His injunctions (1536, 1538) attacked images idolatrously abused, and paved the way for the destruction of altars in the reign of Edward VI. When Henry VIII finally became convinced that his vicegerent was a religious radical who was protecting Protestants secretly, he withdrew his support and allowed Cromwell to fall victim to his conservative opponents. It was not for nothing that the parliamentary bill of attainder against Cromwell charged him in 1540 with heresy as well as treason.

The Dissolution of the Monasteries

Cromwell's most important assignment was the Dissolution of the Monasteries. Probably Henry VIII's main motivation was financial. He needed to annex the monastic estates in order to restore the Crown's finances. He also had to buy the allegiance of the political nation away from Rome and in support of his Reformation by massive injections of new patronage—he must appease the nobility and gentry with a share of the spoils. Thus Cromwell's first task was to conduct an ecclesiastical census, the first major tax record since Domesday Book, to evaluate the condition and wealth of the English Church. The survey was completed in six months, and Cromwell's genius for administration was shown by the fact that *Valor Ecclesiasticus*, as it is known, served both as a record of the value of the monastic assets, and as a report on individual clerical incomes for taxation purposes.

The smaller monasteries were dissolved in 1536; the greater houses followed two years later. The process was interrupted by a formidable northern rebellion, the Pilgrimage of Grace, which was brutally crushed by use of martial law, exemplary public hangings, and a wholesale breaking of Henry's promises to the "pilgrims." But the work of plunder was quickly completed. A total of 560 monastic institutions had been suppressed by November 1539, and lands valued at £132,000 per annum immediately accrued to the Court of Augmentations of the King's Revenue, the new department of state set up by Cromwell to cope with the transfer of resources. Henry's coffers next received £75,000 or so from the sale of gold and silver plate, lead, and other precious items; finally, the monasteries had possessed the right of presentation to about two-fifths of the parochial benefices in England and Wales, and these rights were also added to the Crown's patronage.

The long-term effects of the dissolution have often been debated, and may conveniently be divided into those which were planned, and those not. Within the former category, Henry VIII eliminated the last centers of resistance to his royal supremacy. He founded six new dioceses upon the remains of former monastic buildings and endowments—Peterborough, Gloucester, Oxford, Chester, Bristol, and Westminster, the last-named being abandoned in 1550. The king then reorganized the ex-monastic cathedrals as Cathedrals of the New Foundation, with revised staffs and statutes. Above all, though, the Crown's regular income was almost doubled—but for how long?

The irony of the dissolution was that Henry VIII's colossal military expenditure in the 1540s, together with the laity's demand for a share of the booty, politically irresistible as that was, would so erode the financial gains as to cancel out the benefits of the entire process. Sales of the confiscated lands began even before the suppression of the greater houses was completed, and by 1547 almost two-thirds of the former monastic property had been alienated. Further grants by Edward VI and Queen Mary brought this figure to over three-quarters by 1558. The remaining lands were sold by Elizabeth I and the early Stuarts. It is true that the lands were not given away: out of 1,593 grants in Henry VIII's reign, only 69 were gifts or partly so; the bulk of grants (95.6 percent) represented lands sold at prices based on fresh valuations. But the proceeds of sales were not invested—quite the opposite under Henry VIII. In any case, land was the best investment. The impact of sales upon the non-parliamentary income of the Crown was thus obvious, and there is something to be said for the view that it was Henry VIII's dissipation of the ex-monastic resources that made it harder for his successors to govern England.

Of the unplanned effects of the dissolution, the wholesale destruction of fine Gothic buildings, melting down of medieval metalwork and jewelry, and sacking of libraries were acts of licensed vandalism. The clergy suffered an immediate decline in morale. The number of candidates for ordination dropped sharply; there was little real conviction that Henry VIII's Reformation had anything to do with spiritual life, or with God. The disappearance of the abbots from the House of Lords meant that the ecclesiastical vote had withered away, leaving the laity ascendant in both Houses. With the sale of ex-monastic lands usually went the rights of parochial presentation attached to them, so that local laity obtained the bulk of Church patronage, setting the pattern for the next three centuries. The nobility and gentry, especially moderate-sized gentry families, were the ultimate beneficiaries of the Crown's land sales.

Ruins of the medieval Benedictine abbey at Glastonbury, Somerset, which was sacked during the Dissolution of the Monasteries.

The distribution of national wealth shifted between 1535 and 1558 overwhelmingly in favor of Crown and laity, as against the Church, and appreciably in favor of the nobility and gentry, as against the Crown. Very few new or substantially enlarged private estates were built up solely out of ex-monastic lands by 1558. But if Norfolk is a typical county, the changing pattern of wealth distribution at Elizabeth's accession was that 4.8 percent of the county's manors were possessed by the Crown, 6.5 percent were episcopal or other ecclesiastical manors, 11.4 percent were owned by East Anglian territorial magnates, and 75.4 percent had been acquired by the gentry. In 1535, 2.7 percent of manors had been held by the Crown, 17.2 percent had been owned by the monasteries, 9.4 percent were in the hands of magnates, and 64 percent belonged to gentry families.

Wars and Diplomacy

Without Wolsey or Cromwell to restrain him, Henry resolved to embark on French and Scottish wars, triggering a slow-burning fuse that was extinguished only by the execution of Mary Stuart in February 1587. He turned to war and foreign policy in the final years of his reign, because he felt secure at last. Cromwell had provided the enforcement necessary to protect the supreme head from internal opposition; Jane Seymour had brought forth the male heir to the Tudor throne; Henry was excited about his marriage to Catherine Howard, and had settled Church doctrine by the Act of Six Articles (1539).

The matrimonial adventures of Henry VIII are too familiar to recount again in detail, but an outline may conveniently be given. Anne Boleyn was already pregnant when the king married her, and the future Elizabeth I was born on 7 September 1533. Henry was bitterly

Jane Seymour (Hans Holbein the Younger, c. 1536)

Anne of Cleves (Holbein, c. 1539)

disappointed that she was not the expected son, and when Anne miscarried in January 1536, he was convinced that God had damned his second marriage. He therefore destroyed Anne in a palace coup (May 1536) and married Jane Seymour instead. But Jane's triumph in producing the baby Prince Edward was Pyrrhic, for she died of Tudor surgery 12 days later. Her successor was Anne of Cleves, whom Henry married in January 1540 to win European allies. But Anne, gentle but plain, did not suit; divorce was thus easy, as the union was never consummated. Catherine Howard came next. A high-spirited flirt, she had been a maid of honor to Anne of Cleves, and became Henry's fifth queen in July 1540, a month after the coup that destroyed Cromwell. She was executed in February 1542 for adultery. Finally, Henry took the amiable Catherine Parr to wife in July 1543. Twice widowed, Catherine was a cultivated Erasmian, who did

Possibly Catherine Howard (Holbein, c. 1540)   **Catherine Parr** (unknown artist, c. 1545)

much to preserve the cause of humanist reform until it could re-emerge in the reign of Edward VI.

Henry VIII's new plans for war, which hardened when he learned of Catherine Howard's infidelity, resurrected youthful dreams of French conquests. Wolsey had largely organized the king's early campaigns in 1512 and 1513; Henry led in person a large army from Calais in 1513, seizing Thérouanne and Tournai after the battle of the Spurs (August 16). True, the captured towns were costly to defend and Cromwell called them "ungracious dogholes" in Parliament, but they delighted the king. Another invasion was planned, but Henry's allies were unreliable and Wolsey negotiated an Anglo-French *entente* (August 1514). This crumbled on the death of Louis XII and accession of Francis I (January 1, 1515). But in 1518 Wolsey agreed new terms with France which were transformed

into a dazzling European peace treaty. The pope, emperor, Spain, France, England, Scotland, Venice, Florence, and the Swiss forged, with others, a non-aggression pact with provision for mutual aid in case of hostilities. At a stroke Wolsey made London the center of Europe and Henry VIII its arbiter. This *coup de théâtre* was the more remarkable in that it was the pope's own plan that Wolsey snatched from under his nose. At the Field of Cloth of Gold in 1520, Henry vied with Francis at a vast Renaissance

Having signed a peace treaty with France in 1518, young king Henry VIII would meet Francis I at the Field of Cloth of Gold for a celebrated series of tournaments. This scene by the nineteenth-century artist Friedrich Bouterwek is copied from an original sixteenth-century panoramic painting.

tournament that was hailed as the eighth wonder of the world. Further campaigns in 1522 and 1523 brought Henry's army to within 50 miles of Paris. Then the best chance of all arose: Henry's ally the Emperor Charles V defeated and captured Francis at the battle of Pavia (February 24, 1525). But the opportunity could not be exploited owing to England's financial exhaustion. So Henry made peace with France. And when the divorce campaign began, he became insular in outlook, fearing Catholic invasion. Certainly he was in no position to resume warfare until the reverberations of the Pilgrimage of Grace had died away.

By 1541 Henry was moving towards a renewed amity with Spain against France, but he was prudent enough to hesitate. Tudor security required that, before England went to war with France, no doors should be open to the enemy within Britain itself. This meant an extension of English hegemony within the British Isles—Wales, Ireland, and Scotland. Accordingly Henry undertook, or continued, the wider task of English colonization that was completed by the Act of Union with Scotland (1707).

The union of England and Wales (see map, opposite) had been planned by Cromwell, and was legally accomplished by Parliament in 1536 and 1543. The marcher lordships were shired, English laws and county administration were extended to Wales, and the shires and county boroughs were required to send 24 MPs to Parliament at Westminster. In addition, a refurbished Council of Wales, and new Courts of Great Sessions, were set up to administer the region's defenses and judicial system. Wales was made subject to the full operation of royal writs, and to English principles of land tenure. The Act of 1543 dictated that Welsh customs of tenure and inheritance were to be phased out, and that English rules were to succeed them. Welsh customs persisted in remoter areas until the seventeenth century and beyond, but English customs soon predominated. English language became the fashionable tongue, and Welsh native arts went into decline.

Tudor Irish policy had begun with Henry VII's decision that acts of Parliament made in England were to apply to Ireland, and that the Irish

The union of England and Wales

Parliament could only legislate with the king of England's prior consent. By 1485 English authority did not in practice extend much beyond the Pale (the area around Dublin). But Ireland was generally quiet before 1534, even if the Gaelic chiefs held the balance of power.

The Tudors ruled largely through the Anglo-Irish nobility before the Reformation, but a crisis erupted in 1533 when Irish politics began to merge with those of the Reformation. Surprised by the Kildare revolt (July 1534), Henry VIII could only parley with the rebels until a relief army was organized. Then the defeat of the rebels in August 1535 was followed by a major switch of policy: direct rule. Cromwell's aim was to assimilate Ireland into the unitary realm of England under the control of an English-born deputy, even if this policy required the backing of a standing army controlled from Westminster. Next, Henry VIII changed his style from "lord" to "king" of Ireland (June 1541). His assumption of the kingship was justified on the grounds that "for lack of naming" of sovereignty the Irish had not been as obedient "as they of right and according to their allegiance and bounden duties ought to have been." But the move committed England to a possible full-scale conquest of Ireland, should the chiefs rebel, or should the Irish Reformation, begun by Cromwell, fail. It even militated against the idea of a unitary state. For a subordinate superstructure had been created for Ireland: the later Tudors ruled technically two separate kingdoms, each with its own bureaucracy. In future ideological terms, it became possible to conceive of Anglo-Irish nationalism, as opposed to English or Gaelic civilization. Lastly, despite the confiscation of Kildare's estates and the dissolution by Henry VIII of half the Irish monasteries, the Irish revenues were insufficient to maintain either the Crown's new royal status or its standing army. And since the army could not be withdrawn, the case for the conquest of Ireland was reinforced.

Yet the linchpin of Tudor security was the desire to control Scotland. James IV (1488–1513) had renewed the Auld Alliance with France in 1492 and further provoked Henry VII by offering support for Perkin Warbeck. But the first of the Tudors declined to be distracted, and forged a treaty of Perpetual Peace with Scotland in 1502, followed a year later by the marriage of his daughter, Margaret, to King James. However, James tried to break the treaty shortly after Henry VIII's accession; Henry was on campaign in France, but sent the earl of Surrey northwards, and Surrey decimated the Scots at Flodden on September 9, 1513. The elite

At Flodden Field in Northumberland was fought one of the largest and bloodiest battle in the long history of warfare between England and Scotland. Hampered by weapons and tactics unsuitable for the boggy terrain, 10,000 Scots, including young King James IV, lost their lives on the battlefield. This image from a nineteenth-century history book reflects a later artist's impression of the battle.

of Scotland—the king, 3 bishops, 11 earls, 15 lords, and some 10,000 men—were slain in an attack that was the delayed acme of medieval aggression begun by Edward I and Edward III. The new Scottish king, James V, was an infant, and the English interest was symbolized by his mother, Henry VIII's own sister. But Scottish panic after Flodden had, if anything, confirmed the nation's ties with France, epitomized by the regency of John, duke of Albany, who represented the French cause and urged Francis I to sponsor him in an invasion of England.

The French threat became overt when the mature James V visited France in 1536, and married in quick succession Madeleine, daughter of Francis I, and on her death Mary of Guise. In 1541 James agreed to meet Henry VIII at York, but committed the supreme offence of failing

King James V of Scotland, shown here in a contemporary portrait by an unknown artist, wed Marie de Guise in 1538, securing the French alliance. James died prematurely in 1542 and was succeeded by his infant daughter, later known as Mary, Queen of Scots.

to turn up. By this time, Scotland was indeed a danger to Henry VIII, as its government was dominated by the French faction led by Cardinal Beaton, who symbolized both the Auld Alliance and the threat of papal counterattack. In October 1542 the duke of Norfolk invaded Scotland, at first achieving little. It was the Scottish counterstroke that proved to be a worse disaster even than Flodden. On November 24, 1542, 3,000 English triumphed over 10,000 Scots at Solway Moss—and the news of the disgrace killed James V within a month. Scotland was left hostage to the fortune of Mary Stuart, a baby born only six days before James's death. For England, it seemed to be the answer to a prayer.

Henry VIII and Protector Somerset, who governed England during the early years of Edward VI's minority, nonetheless turned advantage into danger. Twin policies were espoused by which war with France was balanced by intervention in Scotland designed to secure England's back door. In 1543 Henry used the prisoners taken at Solway Moss as the nucleus of an English party in Scotland; he engineered Beaton's overthrow, and forced on the Scots the treaty of Greenwich, which projected union of the Crowns in the form of marriage between Prince Edward and Mary Stuart. At the end of the same year, Henry allied with Spain against France, planning a combined invasion for the following spring. But the invasion, predictably, was not concerted. Henry was deluded by his capture of Boulogne; the emperor made a separate peace with France at Crépi, leaving England's flank exposed. At astronomical cost the war continued until June 1546. Francis I then finally agreed that England could keep Boulogne for eight years, when it was to be restored to France complete with expensive new fortifications. He also abandoned the Scots, endorsing by implication the terms of the treaty of Greenwich. But it was too late: Henry's "rough wooing" of Scotland had already backfired. Beaton had trumped Henry's English party and repudiated the treaty; the earl of Hertford, the future Protector Somerset, was sent north with 12,000 men. Hertford's devastation of the border country, and Lothian, was successful, but was culpably counterproductive. In particular, the sack of Edinburgh united Scottish resistance to English terrorism. Henry VIII had thus engineered exactly what he wished to avoid—simultaneous conflict with France and Scotland. Hertford returned to Scotland in 1545, but the French faction remained ascendant, even after Beaton was murdered in May 1546 by a group of Fife lairds.

The Death of Henry VIII

Henry died in the early hours of January 28, 1547. He had reigned for almost 38 years. On February 8, a solemn dirge was sung in every parish church. Next day a requiem was offered for his soul. On the 14th, his body was transported toward Windsor in a procession four miles long. On the 15th, the corpse was brought to Windsor Castle, where next day it was interred in St. George's Chapel. The king had cheated his enemies. He had successfully defied the pope. He had enlarged the power of the monarchy and established the Church of England. With Wolsey's aid, he had taught the country to punch above its weight in diplomacy. Religious wars had been avoided. The Pilgrimage of Grace had been suppressed and stability maintained. The clergy were subordinated to the secular state. Parliament's power was enhanced, and statute and common law acknowledged as superior to other types of law. A centralized state was in process of formation, as the northern borderlands, Wales, and Ireland were exposed to the power of the Crown. Overseas colonization had been begun. Lastly, the fiscal reach of the state had been extended.

Against this, the Reformation had been left incomplete. The monasteries had been dissolved and the proceeds dissipated in war. More, Fisher, and the London Carthusians had been executed for what was primarily a matter of conscience. It has been said that Henry's vision of himself as an "arbitrator" in the Church of England could turn into a "murderous paranoia," as in 1539 when he burned three evangelical preachers and three papalist Catholics on the same day in order to demonstrate his "impartiality" to the European powers. The case for and against Henry VIII will always be debated. A supreme egoist, who after 1527 allowed passion and not reason to govern his actions, he was still one of the most charismatic rulers to sit on the English throne. The institutions he substantially refashioned (the monarchy, the Church of England, Parliament) still exist in recognizable form. If he is to be judged by the standards applicable to a dynastic monarchy, he was a success, since his children all succeeded to the throne in the order provided in his will.

FOUR

Edward VI

•

THE DEATH OF HENRY VIII left a vacuum at the center. By the terms of the Third Act of Succession (1544), which Parliament approved shortly before Henry left England to lead his army at the siege of Boulogne, the Princesses Mary and Elizabeth were restored to the order of succession after Prince Edward, and it was provided that if the king died before Edward had attained his majority, power would be vested in a regency council to be nominated by Henry in his last will and testament. Edward was aged nine in 1547. As Bacon remarked from the vantage point of the reign of James I, Henry VIII's death was followed by the "strangest variety" of reigns: that of "a child; the offer of an usurpation . . . the reign of a lady married to a foreign Prince; and the reign of a lady solitary and unmarried."

The long-awaited male heir of Henry VIII (by his third wife, Jane Seymour), Edward VI was crowned king of England at the age of nine. Felled by a wasting illness in 1553—most likely tuberculosis—Edward would never reach the age of majority.

Protector Somerset

Minority and female rule were topics that provoked irrational fears and stereotyped impulses in the sixteenth century. The rule of a male minor was easier to accept than that of a woman. The precedents were relatively clear: government would be exercised by a council of regency until the young king was declared "of age." In addition, a protector of the realm or a governor of the king's person might be appointed to pronounce (or perform administratively) the king's will in consultation with the regency council. Such a framework elevated the Privy Council's role in politics, and was likely to stimulate factionalism as leading councilors competed to assume the offices of protector or governor (the two might be held independently or combined). During Henry VI's incapacity in the 1450s, for example, the duke of York's efforts to advance himself and his policies irrespective of the costs to the Crown threatened both the conventions of the monarchy and the interests of his fellow nobles and councilors. In effect, York's actions were the trigger for the Wars of the Roses.

By his will, Henry VIII had appointed a regency council of sixteen members who were to govern the realm and exercise the royal supremacy until Edward was eighteen years old. The council's members were to govern by majority decision. No provision existed in the will for the appointment of a single regent. In the event, the circumstances of Henry VIII's death resembled those of 1509. His death was kept secret for three days while the earl of Hertford secured the person of the young king and seized the remaining assets of Henry VIII stored in the secret jewel houses. On January 31, 1547, the regency council heard Henry VIII's will read and then, apparently unanimously, appointed Hertford to be Protector and Governor of Edward's Person. Within a week, Hertford had overthrown the will with the connivance of William Paget, the dead king's former secretary and the *éminence grise* of the mid-Tudor court. Hertford made himself duke of Somerset and took what (legally) were tantamount to vice-regal powers as Protector, enabling him to issue letters patent and appoint anyone he chose to the Privy Council. To stimulate consent, he further ennobled and rewarded the former members of the regency council with generous grants of land.

Somerset almost certainly had the genuine support of the regency council at first for his role as Protector, even if his brother coveted the post of governor of Edward's person and was executed for conspiracy within two years. But the nobility and other councilors almost certainly imagined that Somerset was merely to be the executive agent of the new regime, and not *de facto* regent. The councilors envisaged that as Protector, Somerset would consult them about key policy decisions, and not attempt to govern as if he were himself the king. In particular, critical decisions about warfare in Scotland and France, about domestic order and security in England and Ireland, and about the advance of the Protestant Reformation were taken by Somerset in ways that his fellow-councilors considered to be arbitrary and ill-informed. It has been said that Somerset was "insecure" in his position because on one level he was a "minister" on the model of Wolsey or Thomas Cromwell, and on another because he lacked the authority of the monarch to bolster him in time of crisis. But his weakness, in reality, stemmed not from his relationship with the boy-king, which was always secure. It was the product of his soured relationship with his fellow-councilors, who believed that, even if he had not usurped the protectorate, he had misled them as to the nature of his intentions. They expected him to seek their advice and report back to them on his actions, whereas Somerset sought to exercise untrammeled power in Edward's name without the constraints of counsel that even Henry VII and Henry VIII had acknowledged. Whereas the Privy Council had always met at Whitehall or another royal palace in the later years of Henry VIII, Somerset summoned councilors, when he finally deigned to receive them, to Somerset House, his new prodigy house in the Strand. The significance of this is not that he was too lazy to ride down the street to Whitehall. It is that he imagined Somerset House as if it *were* the "king's" or the "regent's" official house, and that he himself was quasi-king.

Somerset increasingly played a game of political poker for the highest possible stakes. He snubbed the nobility and gentry, the jealous custodians of traditional social and political authority, and appealed over their

Having heard news of the victory over the Scots at Pinkie, the boy King Edward VI writes in congratulation to his uncle, Duke of Somerset.

heads to the mass of the ordinary people whose milieu lay outside the usual political establishment. In short, he "courted" popularity. It was a ploy that Wolsey—and, in the later years of Elizabeth's reign, the second earl of Essex—also adopted, but on a narrower front and from a far more stable political base than that enjoyed by Somerset.

The Protector quickly discovered that the economic grievances of the ordinary people had become so great by the reign of Edward VI that his overtures to them virtually incited social revolution and a class war. His bid for popularity backfired when the nobility and gentry were unable to contain the large-scale outbreaks of violence and rebellion that sprang mainly from the decline in living standards in the 1540s. Riot and commotion were virtually ubiquitous from 1548 to 1550, save in the north, where memories of the ill-fated Pilgrimage of Grace were perhaps still fresh. Coinage debasements designed to help pay for the French war had caused rampant inflation, and the most abrupt decline in the purchasing power of money coincided with Somerset's enclosure commissions and sheep tax, a platform that confirmed the nobility's worst fears that the Protector supported the poor against the rich. The most serious uprisings took place in Devon and Cornwall, and in East Anglia, culminating in formal sieges of Exeter and Norwich by rebels. Somerset's equivocation, and inability to end this domestic crisis, prompted the earl of Warwick's coup against him in October 1549.

Yet Somerset's most spectacular failure was his continued adherence to the defunct treaty of Greenwich. His desire to realize Henry VIII's plan to subdue French influence in Scotland and achieve the union of the Crowns became an obsession. His victory at the battle of Pinkie (September 10, 1547) was justified as an attempt to free Scotland from the Roman clergy, but the Scottish Reformation was hardly helped by a policy that pushed Scotland ever closer into the embrace of France. In June 1548, 6,000 French troops landed at Leith, and Mary Stuart was removed to France. When Somerset continued to threaten Scotland, Henry II of France declared war on England. Boulogne was blockaded; French forces in Scotland were strengthened. The Scots then agreed that Mary should eventually marry the Dauphin, heir to the French throne. That provision hammered the last nail into Somerset's coffin. Even Paget now deserted him.

Warwick's Coup

The earl of Warwick's coup, and realignment of the Privy Council, was completed by February 1550. Warwick shunned the title of Protector; instead he assumed that of Lord President of the Council, an interesting choice, since it revived an office effectively obsolete since the fall of Edmund Dudley, Warwick's father. Posthumous tradition has vilified Warwick as an evil schemer—a true "Machiavel." But it is hard to see why, for expediency in the interests of stability was the most familiar touchstone of Tudor policy. Three episodes allegedly prove Warwick's criminal cunning: his original coup against Somerset, the subsequent trial which ended in Somerset's execution in January 1552, and the notorious scheme to alter the succession to the throne in favor of Lady Jane Grey, Warwick's daughter-in-law. However, only the last of these charges seems justifiable by Tudor standards, and even this would be regarded differently by historians had the plot to exclude the Catholic Mary actually succeeded.

Warwick, who created himself duke of Northumberland in October 1551, made, in fact, a laudable effort to reverse the destabilization permitted, or left unchecked, by Somerset. Domestic peace was restored by the use of forces which included foreign mercenaries; England's finances were put back on course by means of enlightened reforms and retrenchments. Above all, Somerset's disastrous wars with France and Scotland were quickly terminated. Northumberland sought peace with dishonor—a humiliating but attractive alternative to fighting. Boulogne was returned to France at once; English garrisons in Scotland were withdrawn, and the treaty of Greenwich was quietly forgotten. It thus became inevitable that Mary Stuart would marry the Dauphin, but considerations of age ensured that the union was postponed until April 1558.

Protestant Reform

The English Reformation had meanwhile reached its crossroads. After Thomas Cromwell's execution, Henry VIII had governed the Church of England himself: his doctrinal conservatism was inflexible to the last. But Somerset first obtained the Protectorate as leader of the Protestant faction in the Privy Council, and the young Edward VI mysteriously became a precocious and bigoted Protestant too. In July 1547, Somerset reissued Cromwell's iconoclastic injunctions to the clergy, followed by a Book of Homilies, or specimen sermons, which embodied Protestant doctrines. He summoned Parliament four months later, and the Henrician doctrinal legislation was repealed. At the same time, the chantries were dissolved. These minor foundations existed to sing masses for the souls of their benefactors; as such, they encouraged beliefs in purgatory and the merits of requiems, doctrines which Protestants denied. Somerset thus justified their abolition on religious grounds, but it is plain that he coveted their property even more to finance his Scottish campaigns. Next, the Privy Council wrote to Archbishop Cranmer, ordering the wholesale removal of images

This allegory of the Reformation by an unknown artist depicts Edward VI at his father's deathbed. The Pope lies slumped below, with Edward's Privy Council to the right. The painting on the wall at the top right shows Protestants breaking religious images.

from places of worship, "images which be things not necessary, and without which the churches of Christ continued most godly many years." Shrines, and the jewels and plate inside them, were promptly seized by the Crown; the statues and wall-paintings that decorated English parish churches were mutilated, or covered with whitewash. In 1538 Henry VIII had suppressed shrines which were centers of pilgrimages, notably that of St. Thomas Becket at Canterbury. Protector Somerset finalized the destruction already begun, ensuring that the native art, sculpture, metalwork, and embroidery associated with Catholic ritual were comprehensively wiped out.

The danger was always that Protestant reform would over-reach itself—in the Cornish rebellion of 1549, opposition to the first of Cranmer's Prayer Books provided the chief rallying point. The system for licensing public preachers had broken down by September 1548, and Somerset was obliged, temporarily, to ban all preaching, whether licensed or not, in favor of readings of the official homilies. The Protector, though, promised "an end of all controversies in religion" and "uniform order," and Cranmer also aspired to this ideal. He sought to make England the center of the European Reformation and wrote to Albert Hardenberg, leader of the Bremen Reformed Church:

> We are desirous of setting forth in our churches the true doctrine of God, neither have we any wish to be shifting and unstable, or to deal in ambiguities: but, laying aside all carnal considerations, to transmit to posterity a true and explicit form of doctrine agreeable to the rule of the scriptures; so that there may be set forth among all nations a testimony respecting our doctrine, delivered by the grave authority of learned and pious men; and that all posterity may have a pattern which they may imitate. For the purpose of carrying this important design into effect we have thought it necessary to have the assistance of learned men, who, having compared their opinions together with us, may do away with doctrinal controversies, and establish an entire system of true doctrine.

Protestant theologians who responded to Cranmer's call included John Knox from Scotland, Martin Bucer from Strasbourg, John à Lasco from Poland, Peter Martyr Vermigli from Italy, and Bernardino Ochino,

The reformer Thomas Cranmer, painted by an unknown artist c. 1547–56.

the controversial ex-vicar-general of the Capuchins, who had made a sensational conversion to Protestantism in the early 1540s.

Yet Cranmer was not a radical. By 1550 he had himself become a convert to an uncompromisingly Protestant theology of the Eucharist, but believed that he had an overriding duty to preserve "order and decency" in the Church of England, which meant retaining clerical vestments and many of the rites and ceremonies of the old Catholic liturgies. This was not the view of radical Protestant theologians such as John Knox, to whom Northumberland inadvertently offered the bishopric of Rochester (fortunately Knox refused), or John Hooper, who was appointed bishop of Gloucester, but was soon involved in a public confrontation with Cranmer following his attack on clerical vestments as "rather the habit and vesture of Aaron and the Gentiles, than of the ministers of Christ." Cranmer soon came to see that unity could only be achieved at the price of uniformity—this was the fundamental lesson of the English Reformation. The two editions of Cranmer's Book of Common Prayer (1549, 1552), which enshrined the pure and scriptural doctrines for which the primate had craved, not only had to be approved by Parliament; they had to be enforced by Acts of Uniformity. The advantages from Cranmer's viewpoint were that the Prayer Books were in English, both preserved the traditional clerical vestments, and the second was unambiguously Protestant; the drawback was that they were first published as schedules to the Uniformity Acts, so that the doctrines and ceremonies of the English Church now rested on parliamentary authority, rather than on the independent legislative power of the supreme head. This constitutional amendment marked the final triumph of the Tudor laity over the Church, for Elizabeth I, in fashioning the religious settlement of 1559, took Cranmer's Prayer Books as a precedent.

Jane Grey

Northumberland's patronage of Knox, who in exile during Mary's reign scandalized Europe by theorizing upon the rights of subjects to rebel against idolatrous rulers, illustrates how far the duke had linked his future to the Protestant cause. Edward VI had never enjoyed good health, and by the late spring of 1553 it was plain that he was dying. By right of birth, as well as under Henry VIII's will, Mary, Catherine of Aragon's Catholic daughter, was the lawful successor. But Northumberland's attempted *putsch* in July 1553 needs more than a casual explanation. The facts are that Northumberland bound his family to the throne on May 2 by marrying his eldest son to Lady Jane Grey.

In a painting first exhibited in Paris at the Salon of 1834, Paul Delaroche gives us a nineteenth-century impression of the execution of Lady Jane Grey, queen for nine days in 1553. Delaroche drew his information from a vivid, if apocryphal, report of a sixteenth-century Protestant martyrologist, Jean Crespin.

Jane was the eldest daughter of the marquis of Dorset, and residuary legatee of the Crown, after the Princesses Mary and Elizabeth, under Henry VIII's will. Next, a documentary "device" was drafted, by which Edward VI disinherited his sisters and bequeathed his throne to Jane and her heirs. Edward died on July 6, 1553; Northumberland and the Council proclaimed Jane queen four days later. The duke's treachery seems proved. Yet the plot may have been as much Edward's as Northumberland's responsibility. The "device" was drafted in his own hand, and corrected by him. At the very least, he had been Northumberland's willing collaborator.

Jane Grey ruled for nine days. Knox preached on her behalf, and threatened popery and tyranny should Mary enforce her claim. But the *putsch* was doomed. Mary was allowed to escape to Framlingham, the walled fortress of the Catholic Howard family. Proclaimed by the East Anglian gentry, she marched south. London changed sides; Northumberland, Jane, and their principal adherents eventually went to the block.

FIVE

Philip and Mary

●

MARY TUDOR HAS NOT ENJOYED a good press. History is written by the winners, and in the sixteenth century the winners were the Elizabethan Protestants: the Marian Catholics were losers. Mary was also a female ruler in an age where stereotyped opinion held the government of women to be exceptional and unnatural. Early modern society was patriarchal. Indeed, patriarchy was the most fundamental of the social attitudes of the period, which dictated that fathers should rule. As a result, the posthumous perception of Mary's reputation has often had less to do with her specific actions, or even with the state of religion in the parishes and local communities during her reign, than with Protestant polemic, anti-Spanish xenophobia, and the politics of gender.

Mary was a staunch Catholic, who in 1554 married Philip, son of the Emperor Charles V. Philip himself ruled Spain as regent after 1551, and

This 1554 portrait of Queen Mary is by the Dutch artist Antonis Mor.

succeeded to the sovereignty of Spain, the Netherlands, and the Spanish Habsburg lands in Italy and the New World even while Mary was still alive. Although it became a central plank of the Protestant platform against her, Mary's marriage offered many advantages. By marrying early in her reign, she could expect to deflect the attacks of those who opposed female rule on principle, while her desire, unfulfilled in the event, to have children was an important signal that she took her duty as a dynastic monarch seriously. Of the available prospects, Philip was by far the most eligible spouse: the English candidates for Mary's hand were the scions of obscure noble families, and the notion of marriage to a subject was itself a highly sensitive issue. In the reigns of Henry VII and Henry VIII, England's diplomatic and commercial interests had generally been pro-Habsburg and pro-Netherlandish: the exception was the period of Henry VIII's first divorce. Overall, there is no reason to suppose that Mary's marriage or her Catholicism by themselves were insuperable obstacles to her success. Much of the anti-Spanish and anti-Catholic bias conventionally attributed to her subjects by later historians stems from two sources: Parliament's well-documented fear that Philip would involve England in the Habsburg–Valois wars in Europe, and the religious and commercial rivalries between England and Spain in Elizabeth's reign, which culminated in the Armada of 1588 and were retrospectively mapped onto the Marian era by Protestant church historians.

The Nature of the Marian Dual Monarchy

Mary aimed to preside over a "consensus" government: one from which radical Protestants and the duke of Northumberland's close adherents alone were excluded. In this respect, she did fail, because she had to dictate to her Privy Council each of the three major policies of the reign:

A medal by Jacopo da Trezzo (c. 1555) shows the dual monarchs, Mary and Philip, on either side.

her marriage to King Philip (July 1554), the reunion with Rome (November 1554), and the declaration of war with France (June 1557). On the other hand, she was sufficiently strong as a ruler to get her own way. Her wedding was celebrated at Winchester Cathedral, when she was given in marriage, according to one contemporary account, by the duke of Alva, a leading Spanish nobleman, and according to another account, by the marquis of Winchester and other English nobles. Spanish and English courtiers were carefully intermingled in order of their degrees on the steps of the throne. Large numbers of standards, banners, streamers, and other heraldic devices emblazoned with Spanish and English regalia were commissioned for the occasion, and the public celebrations were lavish and a spectacular success.

The treaties which paved the way for the marriage had been approved in December 1553. They ostensibly favored English interests, since, while Philip was to be king during Mary's lifetime, and the monarchy became, for all practical purposes, a dual monarchy, it was nevertheless provided that Philip had no independent rights to the Crown should Mary die; he was not to exercise rights of patronage independently of his wife; nor was he to take Mary or any of their future children abroad without consent. The treaties were ratified by Parliament in April 1554, when an act was also passed to limit Philip's rights as a husband over his wife and to prescribe that Mary should remain as much "solely and sole queen" after her marriage as she had been before it. But almost as soon as he arrived in England, Philip was accorded precedence over Mary. For example, official documents styled the monarchs: "Philip and Mary by the grace of God King and Queen of England, France, Naples, Jerusalem, and Ireland; Defenders of the Faith; Princes of Spain and Sicily . . ." And at official functions, such as the ceremonies of the Order of the Garter at Windsor, Philip was soon acting as king and sovereign on his own account, a pattern imitated in the subsequent iconography of the monarchy. Whether Philip was merely the "king consort" that had been suggested by the marriage treaties, or had become straightforwardly king in his own right, was decidedly ambiguous. Only when he was absent from the country in Brussels or elsewhere did Mary resume her "sole" authority as ruler: Philip was present in England between July 1554 and August 1555 and between March and July 1557, and absent for the remainder of the reign. After his first departure in 1555, the issue of "absentee" monarchy began to filter onto the political agenda. Furthermore, Philip's reluctance to return after July 1557, when England had finally entered the war against France and it was obvious that Mary would never become pregnant, soured the political atmosphere and became a signal that the effective operation of the dual monarchy was drawing to its close.

The Court of Philip and Mary

Philip was accorded his own royal household. The queen's household was located in what, during her father's and brother's reigns, was the part of the royal palaces usually known as "the king's side"; Philip's court occupied what had formerly been the queen's or consort's apartments, but at the leading palace of Whitehall, these apartments had originally been those of Cardinal Wolsey, and were actually grander and more spacious than the rooms on Mary's side of the court. Whereas Mary's household was relatively small, Philip's must have had difficulty in accommodating itself within the available space. The king brought a full chamber staff with him from Spain only to find another waiting for him in England complete with a guard of 100 archers. A compromise was reached that Philip should use Spaniards almost exclusively in his privy chamber, leaving his English servants to perform outer chamber and ceremonial duties.

If the evidence of public spectacle and the material culture is anything to go by, political and ideological divisions, or any sense of insecurity in the monarchy, were absent in this reign. There was a confident and unreserved commitment to magnificence and the "imagination" of majesty on behalf of the king and queen. Outdoor events and processions were staged on a large scale, and were as dramatic and successful as the indoor ceremonies and entertainments. Vast quantities of luxury goods were requisitioned. Their distribution was not narrowly confined: an inclusive policy was adopted, and as many courtiers as possible cashed in on the perks. Resident ambassadors as well as the nobility, privy councilors, and the lesser members of the royal households received generous allowances. Public ceremonies sought to project the profile of the dual monarchy. The opening of Parliament was preceded by masses and ornate processions involving Spanish as well as English noblemen and courtiers, and elaborate requiems were held for Philip's grandmother, Juana, sometime queen of Castile, in June 1555, and for John III, king of Portugal, in October 1557. Mary revived the ceremony for the blessing of cramp rings on Good Friday. She also touched for scrofula, or "the king's evil," and eagerly participated in the ceremonies for Maundy Thursday in which she washed the feet of a number of poor women corresponding to her age.

Whereas Henry VIII spent an average of £63 on the annual Maundy ceremony, Mary's honor required an outlay of £160.

At the requiem for Queen Juana at St. Paul's Cathedral, the Spanish and English nobility led the solemn procession, walking side by side, headed by the count de Feria and the marquis of Winchester. There followed the imperial, French, Venetian, and Portuguese ambassadors, the clergy, and a small army of mourners carrying banners and escutcheons decorated with gold and silver. A magnificent hearse was constructed of wax over a timber frame with an ornamental dome and gilded canopy. Wax alone for the four staff torches that surrounded the hearse weighed 1,231 pounds, and the event was reminiscent of no lesser an event than the funeral of Henry VIII.

The tomb of the grandmother of Philip II, known as "Juana la Loca," and his grandfather, Philip the Fair.

A comprehensive renovation of furnishings and dynastic symbolism was also set in train. Large sums were spent on embroidered cloths of estate, hangings, heraldic achievements, and badges and accoutrements decorated with the initial letters of the king's and queen's names. Equestrian purchases were prominent, and extra horses, especially geldings and palfreys, were obtained and equipped with pommels of gold and silver. A new royal barge, emblazoned in silver and gold and with elaborate wainscoting, was commissioned, and trimmed with the king and queen's regalia. Finally, building alterations were undertaken at the royal palaces at costs that exceeded anything since the death of Henry VIII apart from the ceremonial fortifications at Greenwich and the improvements to the tournament yard at Westminster begun by the duke of Northumberland. Since these alterations occurred in the calendar years 1554, 1555, and 1557, when Philip's arrival was either imminent or the king was resident in England, it is likely that this expenditure was incurred in adapting the old "queen's" or "consort's side" for his court and entourage. The most significant alterations were undertaken at the palaces of Whitehall, Greenwich, St. James's, Richmond, Eltham, and Hampton Court, and also at Windsor where the Garter ceremonies were convoked.

Philip's Role in Government

It has often been supposed that Philip had no active role in government, and that his interests were confined to the expansion of the royal navy and the defense of the borders in preparation for England's entry into the Habsburg–Valois wars. This is pure myth. His role in politics was unquestioned. As soon as he arrived in England, the lord privy seal, then the earl of Bedford, was instructed to "tell the king the whole state of the Realm, with all things appertaining to the same, as

This portrait of King Philip II of Spain in his royal armor was painted by Juan Pantoja de la Cruz in the late sixteenth century.

much as ye know to be true" and to answer questions on any matter the king wished to discuss "as becometh a faithful councilor to do." Again, two days after the royal marriage was celebrated at Winchester, the Privy Council issued standing orders to its clerks that "a note of all such matters of estate as should pass from hence should be made in Latin or Spanish from henceforth, and the same to be delivered to such as it should please the king's highness to appoint to receive it." State documents of any significance were to be signed by both the king and queen, and a stamp was to be made in both their names for the expedition of lesser matters.

By 1554, an inner circle of councilors associated with Crown policy-making had emerged, but the circle was not co-extensive with the members or most regular attenders at Privy Council meetings. On the contrary, its political weight was derived solely from the relationship of individuals to the king and queen. The circle varied in composition. Usually it comprised the earl of Arundel, the earl of Pembroke, Sir William (now Lord) Paget, and three others. Cardinal Pole, whom Pope Julius III named as his legate to accomplish the reconciliation of England with Rome, and whom Mary appointed archbishop of Canterbury, became a linchpin of the inner circle after his arrival in England. He exerted massive influence on secular as well as religious affairs during the reign, even though he was not a member of the Privy Council. In fact, he was advising Mary by correspondence on the plans for the reunion with Rome from the moment the queen reached London after the collapse of the duke of Northumberland's attempted *putsch*.

As if to crystallize this inner circle, a new tier of conciliar government was established on the day of Philip's first departure from England (August 29, 1555). This was the so-called "Select Council" or "Council of State," a council which was of a distinctively European (and Habsburg) type. Spanish Habsburg practice worked on the basis of regional councils for Castile, Aragon, the Indies, and so on, and departmental councils for war, finance, and the Inquisition, above which sat a policy-making Council of State. It was this last type of council that Philip now envisaged. Its members were to reside at court and to consider "all causes of state and financial causes, and other causes of great moment." They were to report to Philip three times a week, and brief the other councilors on Sundays. Items of immediate concern were preparations for the fourth Parliament of the reign that was due to begin in October 1555, and royal finance, in particular Crown debts and the charges of certain offices in the royal household. A regular correspondence between the

Select Council and Philip on the business of the realm thereafter ensued, which opened with four comprehensive reports submitted by the Council in September 1555.

Although the Select Council did not report to Philip as often as it was meant to, it kept him abreast of the affairs of state almost until the end of the reign. Its reports typically dealt with between three and a dozen subjects; sometimes the original reports were returned to London with Philip's annotations, or else topics were dealt with in correspondence under separate cover. Either way, Philip meticulously studied the Select Council's reports. He sought or received their advice on a wide range of matters: legislation, patronage, and appointments, the nomination and recall of ambassadors, the condition of the regions, the coinage, the appointment of commissioners for tax collection and other social and economic matters, the disputes of foreign merchants, the defense of the realm (especially Portsmouth, Calais, and the Isle of Wight), the activities of English (Protestant) exiles abroad, the state of the borderlands, and relations with Ireland and Scotland. By the summer of 1556, Philip was anxious about threats of domestic revolt, French invasion, and the readiness of the coastal defenses. The Select Council wrote to reassure him, and the earl of Sussex and other nobles and captains were sent to reside in their counties and to take charge of the coastal defenses. When reports were received of a general mobilization in France and of the naval preparations at Dieppe, the earl of Pembroke was dispatched to Calais as lieutenant to assume command of the town and its security. All this shows that Philip was not merely a figurehead or even a "king consort" following his marriage to Mary. He was, and consistently acted as, king of England, even if he was increasingly absent from the realm.

One of the first victims of the Marian Counter-Reformation was John Rogers, shown here being burned at the stake in a 1563 woodcut from Foxe's *Book of Martyrs*.

Marian Counter-Reformation

Mary had set her heart on the reunion with Rome, which after several false starts was achieved in the third Parliament of the reign. Yet she triumphed because she cheated. In the face of the Jane Grey debacle, the Norfolk gentry were persuaded of her Tudor legitimism; they learned the extent of her Catholicism only after she was safely enthroned at Westminster. Even so, we should beware of the bias of John Foxe and other Protestant polemicists writing in Elizabeth's reign, who would prefer us to believe that Mary did nothing but persecute. It is true that Mary burned a minimum of 287 persons after February 1555, and others died in prison. But the leading Protestant martyrs, Bishops Hooper, Ridley, and Latimer, and Archbishop

Cranmer, were as much the victims of straightforward political vengeance. Stephen Gardiner, the failed conservative manipulator of Henry VIII's reign, who had been outwitted by Thomas Cromwell in the 1530s, was abandoned by the king in the 1540s, and had languished in the Tower during Edward's reign, had become lord chancellor in 1553; he had bitter scores to settle. Secondly, we should appreciate that many of the Marian "martyrs" would have been burnt as anabaptists, or Lollards, under Henry VIII. By sixteenth-century standards there was nothing exceptional about Mary's reign of terror beyond the fact that, as in the case of More when he had persecuted Protestants as lord chancellor, she regarded her work as well done. What seemed shocking to contemporaries was that the deaths of the victims occurred within a relatively short space of time (between February 1555 and November 1558), and executions were concentrated in London, the South East, and East Anglia.

The reason for this geographical imbalance is that Protestantism was barely entrenched outside these areas. There was only one burning in the North, five in the South West, and three in Wales. Mid-Tudor Protestantism still embraced no more than 40 percent of the population in London; around 15 percent in the southern and eastern counties; around 25 percent in towns such as Norwich, Bristol, Coventry, and Colchester; and less than 5 percent in the North. Especially significant is that many of the victims were young. Three-quarters of those whose ages can be discovered had reached the age of spiritual discretion—fourteen years—after Henry VIII's break with Rome. They were, therefore, not strictly apostate, since, if they had not known Catholicism, they could not have renounced it.

The law required that it was not simple doctrinal error or genuine ignorance that were punishable, but "obstinate" heresy. Not all the burnings of the Marian martyrs were legal according to canon law itself.

This vindicated the stand of the victims in the eyes of the Protestants, who quoted the Bible: "Out of the mouths of babes and sucklings hast thou ordained strength because of thine enemies." Mary's approach was also seriously undermined when Philip made it clear that he was reluctant to condone a revival of the heresy laws and fresh burnings on the grounds of the resistance that these would incite. Although a devoted Catholic himself, Philip was skeptical of the power of the Inquisition, and was determined to prevent excessive papal interference in his territories. The split between Philip and Mary on this issue was extremely damaging to the queen and to her policy of Counter-Reformation.

In her defense, Mary's true goal was always England's reconciliation with Rome; persecution was a minor aspect of her program. It was thus to her advantage that the parliamentary landed laity were, by this date, thoroughly secular-minded, for they repealed the Henrician and Edwardian religious legislation almost without comment, and re-enacted the heresy laws—all the time their sole condition was that the Church lands taken since 1536 should not be restored. Yet Mary needed papal assistance; she could not work alone. In November 1554, Cardinal Pole landed in England, absolved the kingdom from sin, and proclaimed the reunion. Pole then attempted to implement intelligent ecclesiastical reforms in the spirit of the Counter-Reformation: these covered such areas as the liturgy, clerical manners, education, and episcopal supervision. But his approach was visionary. He saw people not as individuals but as a multitude; he emphasized discipline before preaching; and he sought to be an "indulgent" pastor who relieved his flock of choices they were too foolish to make for themselves. Heresy could not be contained by such methods. Dubbing himself the "Pole Star," Pole thought his mere presence could guide lost souls. And he was afforded neither the time nor the money needed to accomplish his tasks: three years, and virtually no money, were not enough. The ecclesiastical machine ground slowly; standards of clerical education could not be raised without the augmentation of stipends, especially in the north.

Parliament

Parliament by 1553 seemed to have become a relatively compliant institution, largely because the sales of ex-monastic and chantry lands to the laity by Henry VIII and Edward VI had created a structure in which members of the Lords and Commons were virtually shareholders in the Tudor regime. But Mary encountered some difficulties.

First, Parliament thwarted her plans for the coronation of King Philip, which both she and her husband saw as an abject humiliation. Parliament seems to have feared that England would be more likely to be dragged into a European war, or absorbed into the territorial hegemony of the Habsburgs, if Philip were to be anointed and to receive the charismatic and religious approbation that the coronation rites conferred. Next, the desire of Mary and Pole to achieve the reunion with Rome on terms which paved the way for the restoration of the Church lands was comprehensively frustrated by the demands of the nobility and laity. On this occasion, Philip himself was adamant that Parliament's wishes should be respected, since he feared the political consequences of Mary's uncompromising attitude. Thirdly, Parliament refused to confiscate the lands of those 800 or so Protestants who emigrated during the reign to Frankfurt, Zurich, Geneva, and elsewhere. Many of these exiles launched a relentless crusade of anti-Catholic propaganda and subversive literature against Mary, which the government was obliged to suppress or refute as best it could. And yet, despite the vigorous efforts of the Crown, the bill for the seizure of the lands of the exiles was rejected in 1555 by a large majority. Not even the Catholic peers in the

House of Lords were willing to pass the bill without a fight, and it was then thrown out by the Commons. Feelings ran so high that the debates in the Commons almost resulted in fighting, and underhand techniques were used on both sides in the attempt to force the issue. Relations between the Crown and the Commons were soured by this episode, and Sir Anthony Kingston was sent to the Tower by Mary in retaliation.

It would be an exaggeration to say that Parliament "opposed" the Crown in this reign, but it would be correct to conclude that the political consciousness of the laity was enhanced by the clashes over Church lands, and that Parliament expanded its political horizons in defense of what it saw as the interests of the landowning establishment. If a balance sheet is required, Parliament's main success during the reign was to limit Philip's power and protect Elizabeth's claim to the throne; its failure was to prevent England's entry into Philip's war against France in 1557.

Financial Reforms

The reign was, nevertheless, surprisingly successful in other spheres. The financial reforms of Northumberland were completed; the Exchequer was revitalized and reorganized; a blueprint for recoinage was prepared, and was adopted under Elizabeth. In 1557, a committee was named to investigate "why customs and subsidies be greatly diminished and decayed." The outcome was a new Book of Rates in May 1558, which increased customs receipts by 75 percent. Nothing on this scale would be tried again until James I's reign, when the Great Contract of 1610 proved such a disastrous failure.

In the sphere of taxation, the poverty of the Crown in the 1550s led to a fundamental shift both in the theory of taxation and in its focus. Northumberland had appointed William Cecil and Sir Thomas Smith to investigate Crown finances, and they had experimented with new definitions of national or "state" finance. They blurred the traditional distinction between normal and emergency revenue, and argued that taxation was due equally in times of peace and war to meet the regular costs of government. They asserted that subjects had a civic duty to meet the "necessary" expenses of the Crown, and held that the lion's share of ordinary Crown revenue should be raised from excise duties rather than from the proceeds of the Crown lands. Following precedents established in 1534, 1540, and 1543, Northumberland in 1553 and Mary in 1555 levied taxation which subsumed the exceptional needs of defense within the regular needs of government, and justified taxation on the grounds of beneficial rule and necessity. Had this line of thought been carried to its logical conclusion, the fiscal problems of Elizabeth I would have been averted. A revised system of finance might have been constructed on the assumption that the nation should assume responsibility for a national budget indexed to match the needs of population, inflation, and the costs of warfare. But the fiscal philosophy of the mid-Tudor era did not appeal to Elizabeth, who was a conservative in matters of finance. The exception was the emphasis on exploiting customs revenues: the Elizabethan regime increasingly resorted to customs and excise duties, to customs farming, and to selling licenses to concessionary interests for the import or production of consumer goods, in order to compensate for the relative drop in real income derived from the exploitation of the Crown estates.

War and Opposition to the Regime

Mary was the unluckiest of the Tudors. Her reign coincided with an economic and demographic crisis. Harvest failures and severe dearth in 1555–57 caused malnutrition and some starvation. When an influenza epidemic struck in 1556, the death rate soared. The epidemic did not abate until Elizabeth had acceded to the throne. The population dropped by about 200,000, which Protestants interpreted as God's judgment on the regime, and Catholics as retribution for "rebellious murmuring against our regal rulers appointed of God." Rumors of sedition and conspiracy were commonplace. They included reports of putative or failed assassination attempts, claims that Edward VI was still alive, and stories that Mary had either given birth to a monster, or else that a "substitution plot" had been devised. Alice Perwick of London was indicted for saying, "The Queen's Grace is not with child, and another lady should be with child and that lady's child when she is brought in bed should be named the Queen's child."

Yet fears of revolt were not unjustified. In response to Mary's marriage plans, four simultaneous rebellions were orchestrated for 1554, of which Sir Thomas Wyatt's, in Kent, erupted prematurely in January. Wyatt led 3,000 men to London, proclaiming that "we seek no harm to the Queen, but better council and counselors." He declined to pillage the city out of respect for its inhabitants and because Mary's quick reactions had fortified the walls and gatehouses against him. He removed his forces to Kingston—a fatal diversion. His army was defeated, and 100 rebels, including Wyatt himself, were executed. The other risings came to nothing, and what motivated Wyatt and his followers remains uncertain. Fear of a Spanish Habsburg hegemony was clearly part of the rebels' agenda, but since Kent was one of the small number of counties where Protestantism had become firmly entrenched by the death of Edward VI, it is likely that religion was also an important issue for Wyatt's gentry supporters, if not for the rank and file.

A further conspiracy was planned in Elizabeth's favor by Sir Henry Dudley, beginning in July 1555 and ending the following March when the plot was betrayed. Key military officials, such as the captain of Yarmouth Castle, were implicated, as were some leading Protestant gentry. The recurrent theme of the conspiracy was opposition to Philip's coronation. The plan was sketchy and relied almost entirely on luck and opportunity, but came surprisingly close to fruition when the conspirators' attempt to finance themselves and a small invasion force by stealing the bullion in the Exchequer and minting it into counterfeit English coin almost succeeded. The conspirators were supported by the French, and even though the raid on the Exchequer failed, considerable quantities of forged coinage were smuggled into England and put into circulation to disrupt the financial system.

The climax came in March 1557, when Philip sought England's intervention in the war against France. Gardiner, Philip's most ardent supporter in foreign policy, had died in 1555, and apart from Paget (and probably the earls of Arundel and Pembroke) the Privy Council resisted entry into the war. Pressure from Philip, and later from Mary herself, ensured that the decision was finally made. War was declared on June 7, 1557. It began well. Philip secured 7,000 additional troops under the earl of Pembroke. But the war was fought in four theaters. A victory was won at St. Quentin, in which the English forces played a minor role. The battle was considered so important by Philip that it was later depicted in the hall of battles in the Escorial, the new palace and monastery complex that he built close to Madrid between 1563 and 1584.

In England, however, the battle was overshadowed by the costs and dangers incurred in the remaining theaters of war. And mutual trust had collapsed after Philip's second and final departure in July 1557. When the last and greatest disaster of the reign, the loss of Calais, occurred on January 1, 1558, the recriminations were bitter. The town was the last of the former possessions of Henry V that had remained in English hands.

It was attacked by 27,000 French troops across the frozen marshes; the failures of the English defenses had been culpable. The loss of Calais paralyzed the regime. Even Paget abandoned his efforts to support or promote Philip's cause: the morale of the Select Council collapsed. Only Pole and the marquis of Winchester continued to enjoy the king's confidence.

Mary's much-vaunted "pregnancy," meanwhile, proved to be an illusion. Charles de Guise unkindly quipped that she would not have long to wait, "this being the end of the eighth month since her husband left her." Depression had brought the queen almost to a state of despair. Her death in November 1558 was mourned only by her most intimate and Catholic supporters, and the fact that Cardinal Pole died within a few hours of the queen seemed to the Protestants to be an act of divine providence. Henry II of France, meanwhile, exulted with Te Deum and bonfires, and the marriage of Mary Stuart to the Dauphin, the perilous consequence of the aggression of Henry VIII and Protector Somerset, was expedited.

This detail from a 1571 fresco from the Hall of Battles at El Escorial shows three types of weapons—swords, lances, and arquebuses—in use during the Battle of St. Quentin.

SINE SOLE
RIS.

SIX

Elizabeth I

•

ELIZABETH I, DAUGHTER OF Henry VIII and Anne Boleyn, ascended her throne on November 17, 1558. Queen for 44 years, she has won a reputation far in excess of her achievements. It is plain that her own propaganda, the cult of Gloriana, her sheer longevity, the coincidence of the Shakespearian moment, and the defeat of the Armada have beguiled us into ignoring the problems of her reign. Above all, she was high-minded. Sir Robert Naunton was right when he said: "Though very capable of counsel, she was absolute enough in her own resolution, which was apparent even to her last." She controlled her policy; her instinct to power was innate. Councilors attempted to concert their approaches to her on sensitive matters, but they were rarely successful; she would lose her

The **Rainbow Portrait** of Elizabeth I, attributed to Isaac Oliver, c. 1600. Elizabeth holds a rainbow in her right hand, the symbol of peace after storms. The motto reads "Non sine sole iris" (No rainbow without the sun). The ears and eyes depicted on her mantle represent the role of her privy councilors, who listen and watch, but do not pronounce.

temper, whereupon the matter would rest in abeyance. But she postponed important decisions: unless panicked, she could delay for years.

Her attitude has to be offset against her financial position and the conservatism of most of her subjects, who were far from being Protestant "converts" before the outbreak of war with Spain. Possibly her greatest asset was *lack* of preconceptions; she was not a conviction-politician like Sir Francis Walsingham or the earl of Leicester, though her taste for *realpolitik* exceeded Lord Burghley's. Apart from her concern to recover Calais, as revealed by her French campaign of 1562, she ignored conventional royal ambitions. Her father's expansionist dreams were absent; her sister's ideological passions were eschewed; and despite negotiations conducted until 1581, a dynastic marriage was avoided. Although the second half of the sixteenth century saw the rise of ideological coalitions in Europe, England did not possess sufficient resources to wage open war until the 1580s; therefore a passive stance that responded to events as they occurred, while shunning obvious initiatives, was appropriate.

Religious Settlement

At first the emphasis was on religious settlement. The efforts of Northumberland and Mary to reverse the destabilization of 1547–49 were flatly contradictory. Hence Elizabeth's coronation slogan was "concord." Her personal credo remains elusive, but she may originally have aimed to revive Henry VIII's religious legislation, to re-establish her royal supremacy and the break with Rome, and to permit communion in both kinds (bread and wine) after the reformed fashion—but nothing else. If so, she was "bounced" by her chief councilor, William Cecil (later Lord Burghley), for the only time in her reign. When Parliament assembled in January 1559, he introduced bills to re-establish royal supremacy and full Protestant

Elizabeth's chief advisor, Lord Burghley, presides over the Court of Wards and Liveries in this contemporary painting by an unknown English artist.

worship based on the 1552 Prayer Book. And when these were opposed by the Marian bishops and conservative peers, he baited a trap for the Catholics. A disputation was begun at Westminster Abbey (March 31) which restricted debate to what was justified by Scripture alone. When the Catholics walked out, Cecil had a propaganda victory: two bishops were even imprisoned. True, Elizabeth was styled "supreme governor" of the English

Church in an effort to minimize the impact of the supremacy. But when the Acts of Supremacy and Uniformity finally passed, they did so without a single churchman's consent, thereby making constitutional history. The cry of "foul" was taken up by Catholic apologists, who accused Cecil of coercion "partly by violence and partly by fear." Another act returned to the Crown such ex-monastic property as Mary at her own expense had begun to restore to the Church, while a final act strengthened the Crown's estates at the expense of the bishops. The Elizabethan Settlement was completed in 1563, when Convocation approved 39 articles defining the Church of England's doctrine—these were based on 42 articles drafted by Cranmer in Edward VI's reign. Lastly, in 1571, the Settlement gained teeth sharper than the Act of Uniformity, when a Subscription Act required the beneficed clergy to assent to the Thirty-nine Articles.

The Church of England

The Church of England eventually became a pillar of the Elizabethan state. Despite its faults, the framework that John Jewel defended in his *Apology of the Church of England* (1562), and to which the "judicious" Richard Hooker gave rational credibility in *The Laws of Ecclesiastical Polity* (1594–1600), the "Church by law Established" saved England from the religious civil war that afflicted other European countries at the time, notably France. Yet while the Settlement meant that England became officially Protestant in 1559, a huge missionary effort to win the hearts and minds of parishioners (especially those in remoter counties and borderlands) lay ahead. Outside London, the South East, East Anglia, and more populous towns such as Bristol, Coventry, Colchester, and Ipswich, Catholicism predominated at Elizabeth's accession: the bishops and most parochial incumbents were Marians, and committed Protestants were in a minority.

Whereas Elizabeth and Cecil inherited all the negative and destructive elements of Henrician anti-papalism and Edwardian Protestantism, they had inadequate resources to build the reformed Church, though it is false to see their task purely in confessional terms. For by this stage, inertia was strong among those who had come to regard the Church as a rich corporation to be asset-stripped, or as a socio-political nexus whose leaders were local governors and whose festivals characterized the communal year. In addition, Protestantism, with its emphasis on "godly" preaching and Bible study, was an academic creed, unattractive to illiterate villagers steeped in the oral traditions and symbolic ritualism of medieval England.

The decline of Catholicism in the parishes during Elizabeth's reign was due partly to its own internal changes and partly to the success of committed Protestants in marketing a rival evangelical product. One dynamic change sprang from mortality. For the post-Reformation English Catholic community owed everything to Henrician and Marian survivalism, and relatively little to the missions of seminary priests and Jesuits after 1570. Over 225 Marian priests who saw themselves as Roman Catholics and who had lost their positions in the official Church were active in Yorkshire and Lancashire before 1571, supported by a fifth column within the official Church that remained willing to propagandize for Rome. By 1590, however, barely a quarter of the Marian clergy were still alive, and no more than a dozen by 1603. It is important not to forget the conditions in which the Catholics had to work. The penal laws became savage as fears of Spanish invasion increased. In 1584–5, Parliament enacted that if a priest had been ordained by papal authority since 1559, no additional proof was needed to convict him of treason. Furthermore, 123 of the 146 priests executed between the passing of this act and Elizabeth's death were indicted under its terms, and not under those of earlier

This woodcut from a 1563 music book, *The Whole Psalms in Four Parts*, shows a middle-class English Calvinist family in their plain dwelling.

treason laws. But it was the challenge of Protestant evangelism, rather than the threat of persecution, that succeeded in forcing Catholicism into minority status. Protestant evangelism was largely based on preaching, though Elizabeth's personal views and lack of resources precluded a full government program for the propagation of Protestant preaching. What was achieved was often due to voluntary "puritan" efforts. For whereas under Henry VIII and Edward VI the impetus for the Reformation had come largely from the regime, under Elizabeth, by contrast, the "primary thrust" of Protestant evangelism came from below.

A term of abuse, "puritan" was used to index the nature and extent of opinions of which conservatives disapproved. It meant a "church rebel" or "hotter sort" of Protestant; but the core of puritanism lay in the capacity of "godly" Protestants to recognize each other within a corrupt and unregenerate world. Men of conviction, many of them former Marian exiles, the "puritans" sought to extirpate corruption and "popish rituals" from the Church (the cross in baptism, kneeling at the Communion, the wearing of copes and surplices, the use of organs, etc.), but Elizabeth consistently refused to adjust the Settlement even in detail. The most she was prepared to do was to refer petitions of which she approved to the bishops. In fact, when points were tested by puritan clergy, strict conformity was required. Archbishop Parker's *Advertisements* (1566), issued in response to disputes over clerical dress and ceremonies, enforced the rubrics of the Prayer Book. When Edmund Grindal (archbishop of Canterbury, 1576–83), who shared the puritan desire for reformation, dared to tell Elizabeth he was subject to a higher power, he was suspended from office. His successor, John Whitgift (1583–1604), required all clergy to subscribe to the royal supremacy, Prayer Book, and Thirty-nine Articles, or else be deprived.

Marriage and the Succession

The politics of Elizabeth's reign were dominated by the issues of her marriage, the Protestant succession, and the Catholic threat from Europe and Scotland. In the eyes of the Catholic powers, Elizabeth was unfit to rule. She was a woman, unmarried, a heretic, a bastard, and challenged as to her title and right of succession to the English throne by Mary Stuart, queen of Scotland and dowager queen of France. For their part, Cecil and the Privy Council increasingly followed a proactive and radical approach to the political and ideological problems posed by the Reformation, an outlook informed by a keen sense of Protestant providence. Cecil and (later) Walsingham, in particular, believed that the forces of darkness, in particular the papacy, Spain, and the Guise faction in France, were mobilizing against England and that they intended to use Mary Stuart as their instrument. For this reason, the Protestant Reformation had to be disseminated by every available means and Mary Stuart excluded from the succession to the English throne, even if Cecil took a cautious position (compared to Walsingham and the earl of Leicester) on the issue of military intervention in the Netherlands after 1566, where the Dutch Protestants were in revolt against the sovereignty of Philip II of Spain.

Whenever these topics were raised, Elizabeth attempted to forbid or limit discussion or declined to take her privy councilors' advice when it was offered. She even redefined these topics as "matters of state": they became *arcana imperii*—the phrase used in classical literature for the "secrets" or "mysteries of state"; the issues which, if discussed without the sanction of the ruler, pierced the veil of sovereignty. They were the matters that Elizabeth always reserved for her own decision—or more usually indecision—by arguing that she needed to be further "advised" on matters touching her Crown and state, thereby turning recognition of the need for "counsel" into the excuse for rejecting her councilors' advice.

Elizabeth turned her sex to her political advantage. Why she did not marry is a question that has perennially been asked, if rarely answered. Bacon later recalled how she had "allowed herself to be wooed and courted, and even to have love made to her," which "dalliances detracted but little from her fame and nothing at all from her majesty." Her use of "courtship" in the course of working political relationships has, however, been grossly exaggerated. She had four successive "favorites": Robert Dudley, earl of Leicester; Sir Christopher Hatton; Sir Walter Raleigh; and lastly Robert Devereux, second earl of Essex. She flirted with all of them, but Robert Dudley was the only man she ever really wanted to marry. In the first 18 months of the reign, he was rarely absent from court. The Spanish ambassador wrote: "Lord Robert has come so much into favor that he does whatever he likes with affairs and it is even said that her Majesty

Robert Dudley, earl of Leicester, in a posthumous (c. 1609–33) portrait from the workshop of the Dutch artist Jan Antonisz. van Ravesteyn.

visits him in his chamber day and night." By the autumn of 1559, their intimacy was a source of gossip: Robert was already married to Amy Robsart, who was still alive. Probably Elizabeth was in love. There was talk of marriage. The scandal broke in September 1560, when news reached the court that Amy had fallen down the stairs at her home in Cumnor Place, near Oxford. A coroner's jury brought in a verdict of accidental death, but whether Amy died accidentally, or took her own life, has never been proved or explained. Elizabeth hesitated, and then decided that a marriage to Dudley was too dangerous. Only after two years' delay was her favorite admitted to the Privy Council, and he was not ennobled as earl of Leicester until 1564. Elizabeth retained an enduring affection for Dudley: she kept his portrait miniature in her closet, and lovingly preserved his last letter, written shortly before his death in 1588. But their relationship was often turbulent, especially when Dudley acted presumptuously, when the queen would humiliate him, and even exile him from court.

After her brief romance with Dudley, Elizabeth sought to detach her emotions from political considerations. She learned to rule with her head and not her heart. Her marriage became a mere tool of politics and foreign policy. Of her European suitors, only Francis, duke of Anjou, heir to the throne of France in 1579, seemed genuinely to interest her. When the negotiations began, she greeted the duke's agent with a courtesy and coquetry that was unusual. She talked of love rather than of diplomacy or treaties. She entertained him lavishly, and showered him with gifts and love tokens for the duke. When Anjou himself arrived in England, Elizabeth played to perfection the role of a woman in love. She wore Anjou's portrait miniature on her dress, or carried it in her prayer book, and sent him letters and a poetic lament on his departure. Some historians have argued that this was Elizabeth's final fling before the menopause, but this argument rests solely on guesswork. How much was real, and how much a pretence to secure a French *entente* and therefore England's security against the growing threat of Spain, is an issue which can never be resolved.

Otherwise, Elizabeth's courtships were a pretense: they provided the pretexts for straightforwardly diplomatic negotiations. Philip II was the first of her "suitors." There followed Eric XIV, king of Sweden; Adolphus, duke of Holstein; the Archduke Charles of Austria; and Henry, younger brother of Charles IX of France, who later succeeded to the French throne as Henry III (1574–89). (His younger brother, Francis, duke of Anjou, was the final candidate for the queen's hand.) Elizabeth amused herself with these negotiations, and played the candidates off against each other. The archduke was considered between 1563 and

1567, when the Austrian Habsburgs were thought to be more flexible in their Catholicism than was really the case. The diplomacy collapsed when the archduke insisted on celebrating the Catholic mass in the queen's household, which was unacceptable. Exactly the same impediment frustrated the negotiations with France in 1570–71. Elizabeth pursued the idea of a French marriage at this stage for the sole reason that she thought the French would never agree to a defensive *entente* against Spain in the absence of a dynastic marriage. The project failed when Henry demanded the availability of Catholic worship at all seasons of the year.

None of this denies that Elizabeth might have married if the candidate and the terms had been right. It is sometimes claimed that her experiences in childhood and as a young woman had given her an aversion to marriage on principle. She told Parliament in 1559: "This shall be for me sufficient, that a marble stone shall declare that a queen, having reigned such a time, died a virgin." But her statement cannot be taken at face value. She was often forced to react to what she considered to be unreasonable pressure to marry from her (male) privy councilors. She was an instinctive politician and a superb rhetorician. The suggestion that she was unwilling to marry on principle is contradicted by the fact that she came so close to marrying Robert Dudley.

The Catholic Cause

In April 1559, the peace of Cateau-Cambrésis (between Spain, France, and England) ended Mary's French war. During the 1560s, Spain sought to preserve amity with England, not least to ensure free traffic through the English Channel to the Netherlands. Yet Catholics, the papacy, Spain, and France were all potential foes: the real danger was the threat of

The teenage monarchs shortly after they became king and queen of France in 1559: Francis II, the Dauphin of France (age 15) and Mary, Queen of Scots (age 16). This contemporary portrait, after French artist François Clouet, was painted c. 1559.

a Catholic coalition. And by 1569 the Catholic cause was linked to intrigue which, in its more innocent variety, sought to recognize Mary Stuart's right as Elizabeth's successor, but in more dangerous forms plotted to depose Elizabeth and enthrone Mary.

Mary had married the Dauphin in April 1558, and seven months later the Scottish Parliament agreed to offer him the crown matrimonial. Thereafter, the death of the regent, Mary of Guise, unleashed new French intervention in Scotland; there was sporadic fighting, which was overtaken by full-blooded Protestant revolution. When John Knox returned from exile in Geneva to preach at Perth in May 1559, he lit the fuse of a civil war. The Dauphin succeeded to the French throne as Francis II in July 1559, but when he died in December 1560 the Scottish queen was forced to return to Edinburgh—she was back by August 1561. By then Elizabeth and Cecil had intervened decisively on the Protestant side: the Scottish Reformation had become the vehicle for the expulsion of Catholic influence from the British Isles, and the assertion of the hegemony sought by Henry VIII. Mary Stuart's supporters hoped that she would succeed Elizabeth in a Catholic coup, since her grandmother had been Henry VIII's sister, Margaret. But Mary

The Rebellion of Northu: & Westm:

In 1569 the earls of Northumberland and Westmorland plotted to establish the Catholic Mary, Queen of Scots, on the English throne in what would become known as the Northern Rising. The insurrection was easily put down by Elizabeth's forces and more than seven hundred rebels were executed by martial law.

made mistakes in Scotland: she alienated her friends as well as enemies, lost the battle of Langside, and fled to England in May 1568. Elizabeth, in effect, imprisoned her. A chain of intrigues took shape, in which Catholic, papal, and pro-Spanish ambitions allied, threateningly, with factionalism at court. But the Northern Rising of 1569, led by the disillusioned Catholic earls of Northumberland and Westmorland, was incoherently attempted and easily crushed. By 1572, Elizabeth and Cecil had passed another major test. Stability had been preserved: Cecil was ennobled as Lord Burghley.

The Protestant Cause

The Northern Rising and Mary's imprisonment began a new phase in politics. Throughout Europe, opinion was polarizing on religious grounds: England's role as a Protestant champion was central. Relations with Spain deteriorated when Cecil seized Philip II's treasure-ships en route for the Netherlands (December 1568). Then Pope Pius V issued a bull, *Regnans in Excelsis* (February 1570), that declared Elizabeth excommunicated and urged loyal Catholics to depose her. There followed the massacre of Protestants in Paris on St. Bartholomew's Day 1572 and outright revolt in the Netherlands—both fired Protestant consciences and inspired the English to volunteer aid to the Netherlands. Lastly, Elizabeth's defensive *entente* with France was regarded as hostile by Philip II. On these matters the Privy Council was divided. But these divisions were not pro- and anti-Spanish but between *realpolitik* and religion. With few exceptions, privy councilors were united against Spain and committed to the European Protestant cause.

This nineteenth-century painting by Édouard Debat-Ponsan depicts the gruesome scene at the St. Bartholomew's Day Massacre in Paris, where as many as 10,000 French Protestants may have been murdered by a Catholic mob.

In particular, Burghley, the earl of Sussex, Leicester, and Walsingham agreed on the broad aims of a Protestant foreign policy in the 1570s and 1580s. Their differences centered only on the extent to which England should become militarily committed. Leicester and Walsingham wanted direct English intervention in the Netherlands, but the queen and Burghley were adamant that England alone could not survive war with Spain.

Yet when war with Spain came in 1585, England was isolated. After 1572 Elizabeth assisted France against Spain in the Netherlands, trying to reconcile conflicting political, religious, and commercial interests at minimum cost. She backed an intervention in the Netherlands by Francis, duke of Anjou, her most plausible suitor. But Anjou died in June 1584 having failed to halt Spanish power. And since the Protestant Henry of Navarre now became heir to the French throne, the Wars of Religion resumed in France: the Guise party allied with Spain (secret treaty of Joinville, December 1584). So France was divided while Philip II prospered. He annexed Portugal (1580) and the Azores (1582–83): the size of his combined fleets exceeded those of the Netherlands and England combined. At this point the marquis of Santa Cruz proposed the "Enterprise of England"—an Armada to overthrow Elizabeth. Observers debated only whether the Netherlands or England would be reduced first.

The pivotal event was the assassination of the Dutch leader, William of Orange (July 10, 1584). This created panic among English politicians who feared that Elizabeth, too, might fall victim. In May 1585, Philip felt confident enough to seize all English ships in Iberian ports; Elizabeth responded by giving Leicester his head, allying with the Dutch States General in August, and dispatching the earl to Holland with an army. But Leicester's mission was a fiasco; his ignominious return in

December 1587 was shortly followed by his death. Only Sir Francis Drake and other naval freebooters enjoyed success. And outright war followed Mary Stuart's execution in February 1587. For new Catholic plots, at least one of which involved Elizabeth's attempted assassination, hardened the Privy Council's attitude. Elizabeth stood indecisive and immobile; Mary had been tried and convicted, but she was of the royal blood. Elizabeth repudiated regicide. But the Council could wait no

After nineteen years of imprisonment, Mary, Queen of Scots, was executed in 1587. Her tomb is in Westminster Abbey.

longer: the sentence was put into effect. Scotland fulminated, but the 21-year-old James VI was appeased by subsidies and enhanced prospects of the greatest of glittering prizes—succession to the English Crown.

The Armada was sighted off the Scilly Isles on July 19, 1588: the objective was the conquest of England, which would itself assure the reconquest of the Netherlands. Philip's plan was to win control of the English Channel, to rendezvous with the duke of Parma off the coast of Holland, and to transport the crack troops of Philip's Army of Flanders to England. The main fleet was to cover Parma's crossing, and then unite forces carried by the Armada itself with Parma's army in a combined invasion of England. The Armada was commanded by the duke of Medina Sidonia; the English fleet was led by Lord Howard of Effingham, with Drake as second in command. Effingham sailed in the *Ark Royal*, built for Sir Walter Raleigh in 1581; Drake captained the *Revenge*, commissioned in 1575. In England the local militias were mobilized; possible landing places were mapped, and their defenses strengthened. But had Parma landed, his army would have decimated English resistance: the effectiveness of English sea-power was vital.

Vertooninge van de ontsachlyke Spaansche Krygs vloot, in den Jaare 1588.

The Dutch artist Jan Luyken captures the Spanish Armada at sea in this 1679 engraving.

In the event, the defeat of the Armada was not far removed from traditional legend, romantic games of bowls excepted. The key to the battle was artillery: the Armada carried only 19 or 20 full cannon and its 173 medium-heavy and medium guns were ineffective—some exploded on use, which suggests that they were untested. And whereas the Spanish had only 21 culverins (long-range iron guns), the English had 153; whereas the Spanish had 151 demi-culverins, the English had 344. In brief, Effingham and Drake outsailed and outgunned their opponents. The battered Armada fled north toward the Firth of Forth, trailing back to Spain via the Orkneys and the west coast of Ireland. In August 1588 Protestant England celebrated with prayers and public thanksgiving. But the escape was narrow; Elizabeth never again committed her whole fleet in battle at once. Moreover, although later generations boasted that she kept Spain at bay at minimum cost by avoiding foreign alliances and relying on the royal navy and part-time privateers who preyed on enemy shipping, the supremacy of the naval over the Continental land war is a myth. The war at sea was only part of a struggle that gripped the whole of Western Europe and centered on the French civil war and revolt of the Netherlands. Since Elizabeth lacked the land forces, money, and manpower to rival Spain, she was obliged to help Navarre and the Dutch. The Catholic League was strongest in Picardy, Normandy, and Brittany; these regions and the Netherlands formed what amounted to a continuous war zone. Elizabeth dispatched auxiliary forces annually to France and the Netherlands in 1589–95; cash subsidies apart from the cost of equipping and paying these troops cost her over £1 million. By comparison, English naval operations were heroic sideshows of mixed strategic value.

Elizabeth's Later Years

Late Elizabethan policy was damaging from several viewpoints. The aims of Navarre and his partners diverged, and when in July 1593 he converted to Catholicism to secure his throne as Henry IV, he soured hopes of a European Protestant coalition. Elizabeth, however, continued to support him, since a united France restored the balance of power in Europe, while his debts to the queen ensured continued collaboration in the short term. Next, the English quarreled with the Dutch over their mounting debts and the cost of English garrisons and auxiliary forces. Thirdly, the cost of the war was unprecedented in English history: even with parliamentary subsidies, it could only be met by borrowing and by sales of Crown lands. Lastly, the war, in effect, spread to Ireland. The Irish Reformation had not succeeded: Spanish invasions as dangerous as the Armada were attempted there. These, combined with serious internal revolt, obliged the Privy Council to think in terms of the full-scale conquest of Ireland logically induced by Henry VIII's assumption of the kingship. Elizabeth hesitated—as well she might. At last her favorite, the dazzling but paranoid earl of Essex, was dispatched in 1599 with a large army. But Essex's failure surpassed even Leicester's in the Netherlands; he deserted his post in a last-ditch attempt to salvage his career by personal magnetism, and was executed in February 1601 for leading his faction in a desperate rebellion through the streets of London. Lord Mountjoy replaced him in Ireland, reducing the Gaelic chiefs to submission and routing a Spanish invasion force in 1601. The conquest of Ireland was completed by 1603. The results were inherently contradictory. English hegemony was confirmed, but the very fact of conquest alienated the Gaelic population and vanquished hopes of advancing the Irish Reformation, and thus achieving cultural unity with England.

Such contradictions were not confined to Irish history. The most obvious area of decline was that of government. Did Elizabethan institutions succumb to decay during the war with Spain? Criticism centers on the inadequacy of taxation, local government, and military recruitment; the rise of corruption in central administration; the abuse of royal prerogative to grant lucrative "monopolies" or licenses in favor of courtiers and their clients, who might also enforce certain statutes for profit; and the claim that the benefits of the Poor Laws were negligible in relation to the rise in population and scale of economic distress in the 1590s.

Problems of Government

Elizabeth allowed the taxation system to decline. Not only did the value of a parliamentary subsidy fail to increase in line with inflation despite soaring levels of government expenditure, but receipts dropped in cash terms owing to static tax assessments and widespread evasion. Rates became stereotyped, while the basis of assessment became the taxpayer's unsworn declaration. Whereas Wolsey had attempted to tax wage-earners as well as landowners in Henry VIII's reign, Elizabeth largely abandoned the effort. Although the yield of a subsidy was £140,000 at the beginning of her reign, it was only £80,000 at the end. Burghley himself evaded tax, despite holding office as Lord Treasurer after 1572. He grumbled hypocritically in Parliament about tax cheating, but kept his own assessment of income static at £133 6s. 8d.—his real income was approximately £4,000 per annum. Lord North admitted that few taxpayers were assessed at more than one-sixth or one-tenth of their true wealth, "and many be 20 times, some 30, and some much more worth than they be set at, which

Queen Elizabeth I, sitting beneath her "Cloth of Estate" in the House of Lords, presides over Parliament in this contemporary engraving.

the commissioner cannot without oath help." When arguing in Parliament for exemption of lesser taxpayers in 1601, Raleigh suggested that while the wealth of a person valued in the subsidy books at £3 per annum was close to his true worth, "our estates that be £30 or £40 in the Queen's books are not the hundredth part of our wealth."

The failure of the regime to maintain the yield of the subsidy was the biggest weakness of the late Tudor state. Admittedly, local taxation escalated, especially for poor relief, road and bridge repairs, and militia expenditure. The recruitment and training of the militia was very expensive and burdened the localities with additional rates. Training cost considerable sums by the 1580s; the localities were responsible, too, for providing stocks of parish arms and armor; for paying muster-masters; for repairing coastal forts and building beacons; and for issuing troops mustered for the foreign service with weapons and uniforms, as well as conveying them to the required port of embarkation. In Kent the cost of military preparations borne by the county between 1585 and 1603 exceeded £10,000. True, a proportion of "coat-and-conduct" money required to equip and transport troops was recoverable from the Exchequer, but in practice the localities met roughly three-quarters of the cost. Also, whereas merchant ships (except customarily fishing vessels) had traditionally been requisitioned from coastal towns and counties to augment the royal navy in time of war, the Crown in the 1590s started demanding money as well as ships, and impressed fishermen for service in the royal navy and aboard privateers to the detriment of the local economy. When the ship money rate was extended to inland areas such as the West Riding of Yorkshire, it aroused opposition to the point where the Crown's right to impose it was questioned.

The strain of a war economy was cumulative. Conscription became a flashpoint as 105,800 men were impressed for military service in the Netherlands, France, Portugal, and Ireland during the last eighteen years of the reign. Conscription for Ireland after 1595 aroused the greatest resentment. In 1600 there was a near mutiny of Kentish cavalry at Chester as they traveled to Ulster. Pressure on the counties led to administrative breakdowns and opposition to central government's demands, while disruption of trade, outbreaks of plague (much of it imported by soldiers returning from abroad), ruined harvests in 1596 and 1597, and acute economic depression caused widespread distress.

At the level of central government, rising corruption signaled a drift toward venality. The shortage of Crown patronage during the long war and the logjam in promotion prospects encouraged a traffic in offices. Competition at court created a "black market" in which influence was bought and sold. Offices were overtly traded, but unlike Henry VII's sales, they rarely benefited the Crown financially. Payments were made instead to courtiers to influence the queen's choice. For a minor post £200 or so would be offered, with competitive bids of £1,000 to £4,000 taken for such lucrative offices as the receivership of the court of wards or treasurership at war. And bids were investments, since if an appointment resulted, the new incumbent would so exercise his office as to recoup his outlay plus interest, for which reason the system was corrupt by Tudor as well as modern standards, because the public interest was sacrificed to private gain.

Where late Elizabethan government aroused the most overt dissent was in the matters of licenses and monopolies. Clashes in 1597 and 1601 were the ugliest in Parliament during the Tudor period. They signaled unequivocal resentment of abuses promoted by courtiers and government officials. True, some monopolies or licenses were genuine patents or copyrights, while others established trading companies with overseas bases which also provided valuable consular services for merchants abroad. But many were designed simply to corner the market in commodities for the patentees, or to grant them exclusive rights which enabled them to demand payments from manufacturers or tradesmen for carrying out their legitimate businesses. They had doubled the price of steel; tripled that of starch; caused that of imported glasses to rise fourfold, and that of salt elevenfold. Courtiers enforced them with impunity, since patents rested on royal prerogative—the common law courts lacked the power to vet them without royal assent. Indignation was first vented in Parliament in the 1570s, but it was the late Elizabethan explosion of monopolies that provoked the backlash. When the young lawyer, William Hakewill, cried, "Is not bread there?", Elizabeth had personally to intervene to neutralize the attack. In 1601 she averted the crisis at the expense of the patentees: a proclamation annulled 12 monopolies condemned in Parliament and authorized subjects grieved by other patents to seek redress in the courts of common law.

The Poor Laws

The final criticism leveled against late Elizabethan government is that the benefits of the Poor Laws were crushed by the rise of population and economic distress of the 1590s. Although this question raises problems, a Malthusian diagnosis can be eliminated. The Elizabethan state profited from a steadily rising birth rate that coincided with increased life expectancy. In particular, mortality crises of

1586–87 and 1594–98 were regional rather than national. The death rate jumped by 21 percent in 1596–97, and by a further 5 percent in 1597–98. But fewer parishes experienced crisis mortality than during the influenza epidemic of 1555–59. And later economic depressions in 1625–26 and 1638–39 were more severe. On the other hand, agricultural prices climbed higher in real terms in 1594–98 than at any time before 1615, while real wages plunged lower in 1597 than at any time between 1260 and 1950. Perhaps two-fifths of the population fell below the margin of subsistence: malnutrition reached the point of starvation in the uplands of Cumbria; disease spread unchecked; reported crimes against property increased; and thousands of families were thrown on to parish relief.

Legislation was enacted in 1572, 1598, and 1601 for the punishment of vagrancy and the relief of the poor. Parliament instituted a national scheme of compulsory parish rates to relieve the aged and dependent poor, while raw materials such as wool, flax, hemp, and iron were to be purchased upon which the able-bodied unemployed could be set to work—this began the system of poor relief and local rates which remained in force until the Poor Law Amendment Act of 1834. But in a material sense, the legislation was inadequate when inflation and the rise in prices are factored into the account. The estimated cash yield of endowed charities for poor relief by 1600 totaled £11,700 per annum—one-quarter of 1 percent of national income. Yet the estimated amount raised by poor rates was smaller. If these figures are correct, what was audible was not a bang but a whimper. At a different level the Poor Laws operated as a placebo: the "laboring poor" were persuaded that their social superiors shared their view of the social order and denounced the same "caterpillars of the commonwealth"—chiefly middlemen.

Domestic Architecture

The years from 1570 to 1610 mark the first key phase of the English housing revolution. Probate inventories suggest that from 1530 to 1569 the average size of the ordinary middle-class house was three rooms. Between 1570 and the end of Elizabeth's reign it was four or five rooms. The period 1610–42, which was the second phase of the revolution, saw the figure rise to six or more rooms. After 1570, prosperous yeomen might have six, seven, or eight rooms; husbandmen might aspire to two or three rooms, as opposed to the one-room cottages common in 1500. Richer farmers would build a chamber over the open hall, replacing the open hearth with a chimney stack. Poorer people favored ground-floor extensions: a kitchen, or second bedchamber, would be added to an existing cottage. Kitchens were often separate buildings to reduce the risk of fire. A typical late Elizabethan farmstead might be described as "one dwelling house of three bays, one barn of three bays, one kitchen of one bay." Meanwhile there were corresponding improvements in domestic comfort. The average investment in hard and soft furniture, tableware, and kitchenware before 1570 was around £7. Between 1570 and 1603 it rose to £10 10*s* (£10.5), and in the early Stuart period it climbed to £17. The value of household goods of wealthier families rose by 250 percent between 1570 and 1610, and that of middling and lesser persons slightly exceeded even that high figure. These percentages were in excess of the inflation rate.

In the higher echelons of Tudor society, manor and prodigy houses were characterized by increased luxury and comfort. Architecture after about 1580 was inspired by medieval ideals of chivalry as much as by Renaissance classicism. The acres of glass and towering symmetry of

Holbein's design for a fireplace for Henry VIII, 1540. This fine example was perhaps intended for Bridewell Palace.

An avenue in the gardens at the side of Hardwick Hall, the Elizabethan "prodigy house" in Derbyshire.

Hardwick New Hall, Derbyshire, built in 1591–97 by Robert Smythson for Elizabeth, countess of Shrewsbury, paid homage to both the Gothic and classical traditions. But if Elizabethan Gothic architecture was neo-medieval in its outward profile, the aim was for enhanced luxury within. In any case, the neo-medieval courtyards, gatehouses, moats, parapets, towers, and turrets of Tudor prodigy houses were ornamental, not utilitarian. The parapets at Hardwick incorporated the initials "E.S." (Elizabeth Shrewsbury)—the decorative device that proclaimed the parvenue. Brick chimneys became a familiar feature, which signified the arrival of the kitchen and service quarters within the main house, into either a wing or a semi-basement. As time progressed, basement services became fairly common, and were particularly favored in town houses built on restricted sites. Household servants began to be relegated to the subterranean caverns from which it took three centuries to rescue them.

The characteristic feature of the Elizabethan manor house was the long gallery, hung with historical portraits, where private conversations could be conducted without constant interruption from the traffic of servants. These long galleries were modeled on those erected in the royal palaces earlier in the century. An early example was the gallery at Hampton Court, where in 1527 Henry VIII and Sir Thomas More had paced uneasily together as they first discussed the terms of the king's proposed divorce. In similar fashion, ground-floor parlors replaced the great hall as the customary family sitting and dining rooms—at least for normal daily purposes. The family lived in the ground-floor parlors and the first-floor chambers; the servants worked on both these floors and in the basement, and slept in the attics or turrets. Staircases were revitalized as a result: the timber-framed structure gradually became an architectural feature in itself. Finally, provision of fresh-water supplies and improved sanitary arrangements reflected the Renaissance concern with private and public health. In the case of town houses, the family would often go to immense lengths to solve drainage problems, sometimes paying a cash composition to the municipal authorities, but frequently performing some service for the town at court or in Parliament in return for unlimited water or drainage.

Miniature portraits by Nicholas Hilliard (1547–1619), probably of Henry Percy, ninth earl of Northumberland, c.1595 (top), and (bottom) of Sir Walter Raleigh, c. 1585. Hilliard was the most important artist of the Elizabethan period. His style was based on Holbein's, but he was also influenced by French court portraiture. He believed that the face was the mirror of the soul. This portrait of Northumberland is a rare example of a Hilliard miniature in which the sitter is placed out of doors in the world of nature.

Art and Music

Hilliard became the most influential painter at the Elizabethan court on the strength of his ravishing miniatures. Trained as a goldsmith, Hilliard earned renown for his techniques as a "limner," or illuminator of portrait gems that captured the "lovely graces, witty smilings, and these stolen glances which suddenly like lightning pass, and another countenance taketh place." Intimacy was the key to this style, combined with a wealth of emblematic allusion that added intellectual depth to the mirror-like image portrayals. In Hilliard's hands, the miniature was far more than a mere reduced version of a panel portrait—but that was thanks to his creative invention. To enhance the techniques learned in the workshops of Ghent and Bruges, where the miniature was painted on fine vellum and pasted on to card, Hilliard used gold as a metal, burnishing it "with a pretty little tooth of some ferret or stoat or other wild little beast." Diamond effects were simulated with utter conviction, and Hilliard's jewel-bedecked lockets were often worn as badges, or exchanged as pledges of love between sovereign and subject or knight and lady. Hilliard's techniques were passed on to his pupil, Isaac Oliver, and finally to Samuel Cooper. The miniature was ultimately confounded by the invention of photography.

Music was invigorated by royal and noble patronage, by the continued liturgical demands of the Church, and by the steady abandonment of the modal limitations of the medieval style in favor of more audacious and harmonious techniques of composition and performance. The Tudor monarchs, together with Cardinal Wolsey, were distinguished patrons of music both sacred and secular. An inventory of Henry VIII's musical instruments suggests that as lavish a selection was available in England as anywhere in Europe—the king himself favored the lute and organ. His and Wolsey's private chapels competed to recruit the best organists and singers. In Mary's reign, England was exposed to the potent artistry of Flemish and Spanish music, while the seminal influence of Italy was always present in the shape of Palestrina's motets and the works of the Florentine madrigalists. Elizabeth I retained a large corps of court musicians drawn from Italy, Germany, France, and England itself. But her Chapel Royal was the premier conservatoire of musical talent and invention, since Thomas Tallis, William Byrd, and John Bull made

The centrality of music to the Tudor "Renaissance man" is symbolized by the lute and flutes in this detail from Holbein's *The Ambassadors* (1533).

their careers there. The Protestant Reformation happily encouraged, rather than abandoned, composers—the Edwardian and Elizabethan injunctions left liturgical music intact, and many of the gentlemen of the Chapel discreetly remained Catholics, including Byrd and Bull. Yet it was the technical advances that really mattered. Byrd and Bull freed themselves from the old ecclesiastical modes, or ancient scales. Tallis and Byrd gained a license for music printing that enabled them to pioneer printed musical notation in collaboration with an established printer. Melody, harmony, and rhythm became as important to music as plainsong and counterpoint, and the arts of ornamentation and virtuoso extemporization thrived among the virginalists, and among the lute and consort players.

Literature

Erasmus's wit and More's satirical fiction expressed (though in Latin) the intellectual exuberance of pre-Reformation Europe. The pioneers of classical idioms in English vernacular literature were Sir Thomas Elyot, Sir John Cheke, and Roger Ascham. Next, Sir Thomas Wyatt, Henry Howard, earl of Surrey, and Sir Philip Sidney reanimated English lyric poetry and rekindled the sonnet as the vehicle of eloquent and classical creativity. But it was Edmund Spenser who rediscovered what English prosody had lacked since the time of Chaucer. Once again, music tutored the ear, and the connections between ear and tongue were fully realized. Spenser attained an impeccable mastery of rhythm, time, and tune—his work was no mere "imitation of the ancients." In particular, his blend of northern and midland with southern dialects permitted verbal modulations and changes of diction and mood akin to those of lute players. His pastoral sequence, *The Shepheards Calendar* (1579), was a landmark in the history of English poetry, its melodious strains encapsulating the pains and pleasures of pastoral life:

> Colin, to heare thy rymes and roundelayes,
> Which thou wert wont on wastfull hylls to singe,
> I more delight then larke in Sommer dayes;
> Whose Echo made the neyghbour groves to ring,
> And taught the byrds, which in the lower spring
> Did shroude in shady leaves from sonny rayes,
> Frame to thy songe their cherefull cheriping,
> Or hold theyr peace, for shame of thy swete layes.

Spenser's masterpiece was *The Faerie Queene* (1589 and 1596), an epic poem, which examined on a dazzling multiplicity of levels the nature and quality of the late Elizabethan polity. The form of the poem was Gothic as much as Renaissance: details took on their own importance, decorating the external symmetry without damaging the total effect. The work was above all, though, an allegory. As Spenser explained in a dedicatory epistle to Sir Walter Raleigh, "In that Fairy Queen I mean glory in my general intention, but in my particular I conceive the most excellent and glorious person of our sovereign the Queen, and her kingdom in Fairy land. And yet, in some places else, I do otherwise shadow her." The allegory was part moral, part fictional—there was no easy or straightforward correspondence of meaning. Yet it had a single end; like *Piers Plowman* before it, and *Pilgrim's Progress* afterwards, *The Faerie Queene* led the reader along the path upon which truth was distinguishable from falsehood. To this end, the ambition, corruption, intrigue, and secular-mindedness of Elizabethan power politics were sublimated into the "delightful land of Faerie," clothed in the idyllic garments of romance, and exalted as the fictional realization of the golden age of Gloriana.

The poem failed to impress the Elizabethan establishment. Spenser informed Raleigh that his "general end" was "to fashion a gentleman or noble person in virtuous and gentle discipline." Yet the ambiguities were pervasive. Chivalry had been soured by Renaissance politics and statecraft; the "verray parfit, gentil knyght" of Chaucer's age had been displaced by the Machiavellian courtier. The golden age had passed, if it had ever existed:

> So oft as I with state of present time
> The image of the antique world compare,
> When as mans age was in his freshest prime,
> And the first blossome of faire vertue bare;

Such oddes I finde twixt those, and these which are,

As that, through long continuance of his course,

Me seemes the world is runne quite out of square

From the first point of his appointed sourse;

And being once amisse growes daily wourse and wourse.

Spenser's allegory in *The Faerie Queene* was unquestionably over-complex; his attempt to fuse worldly and idealized principles of behavior into a single dramatic epic was bound to prove unmanageable. Moreover, the reader was obliged to unriddle endless personifications of Elizabeth as the moon-goddess, Diana (or Cynthia or Belphoebe), of Sir Walter Raleigh as Timias, of Mary Stuart as Duessa, who also doubled as Theological Falsehood—and so on. However, Spenser's failure to convince, as opposed to his poetic ability to delight, actually *heightens* our impression of his disillusion. We are taught to debunk the myth of Gloriana; art has held "the mirror up to nature" and shown "the very age and body of the time his form and pressure."

The most celebrated and accomplished Tudor writer was, of course, William Shakespeare. Author of 38 plays that included *Hamlet* (1600–1), *King Lear* (1605–6), and *Othello* (1604), and of 154 sonnets (1593–97), together with *Venus and Adonis* and *The Rape of Lucrece* (1593–94), he has exerted greater influence on English literature and drama than any other individual writer. The sheer vitality, power, and virtuosity of his work remain unmatched in any European language; his genius exceeded that of Chaucer or Tennyson—it need not be justified or explained. We should, however, remember that Shakespeare was not an "intellectual" or "elitist" writer, like Milton or Voltaire. His orbit centered on Stratford and London, not Oxford and Cambridge. His was the everyday world of

A CATALOGVE

of the feuerall Comedies, Hiftories, and Tra-
gedies contained in this Volume.

The first collected edition of Shakespeare's plays, commonly called the First Folio, was printed in 1623. Only about a quarter of the estimated 1,000 copies printed have survived to modern times, making it one of the most valuable books printed in English. The largest extant collection is in the Folger Shakespeare Library in Washington, DC.

life, death, money, passion, stage business, and the alehouse—such matters became the stuff of peerless drama and poetry. The rich variety of his experience is perhaps the chief reason for the universality of his appeal; certainly there is no hint of the bigot or intellectual snob in his work.

His experience was that of a writer at a cultural crossroads. After about 1580, European literature explored increasingly the modes of individual expression and characterization associated with modern processes of thought. Authors and the fictional characters they created displayed awareness both of experience in general, and of themselves as the particular agents of unique experiences. Shakespeare's *Hamlet* and Christopher Marlowe's *Doctor Faustus* (1592) illustrate the dramatic depiction of individual experience in Elizabethan literature. Of the two plays, *Hamlet* is the more advanced. Shakespeare took a familiar plot and transformed it into a timeless masterpiece. But Marlowe's *Faustus* was not far behind. Both dramatists were eager to pursue psychology, rather than ethics. The difference is that Faustus does not pass beyond the bounds of egotism and self-dramatization to realize self-analysis, whereas Hamlet's subjective introspection and self-doubts are the keystones of the action:

> What a piece of work is a man! how noble in reason! how infinite in faculties! in form and moving, how express and admirable! in action, how like an angel! in apprehension, how like a god! the beauty of the world! the paragon of animals! And yet to me, what is this quintessence of dust?
>
> *(Hamlet, II. ii. 323–9)*

Late medieval philosophy had dealt with the objective appreciation of senses, natures, and truth—this reflected the scholastic cast of mind. By the

1590s, the emphasis had shifted towards subjectivity and self-expression, paradoxically under the influence of Calvinist theology, which so stressed the inflexibility of God's predestined Word that a person's quest for grace necessarily came to depend on systematic self-scrutiny.

Marlowe and Shakespeare dominated late Elizabethan drama, although they did not monopolize it. The allegories and morality plays of the fifteenth century flourished until suppressed, especially in such towns as Chester, Coventry, and York. But the Brave New World was symbolized by Shakespeare's Globe Theatre in London, where the impact of the Protestant Reformation had combined with the sophistication of metropolitan life to give distinctive shape to the preferred drama of modern Britain. Self-expression, individuality, and the soliloquy were the cultural developments that paralleled the expansion of education and literacy, the birth of the nonconformist conscience, and the growth of cosmopolitan attitudes.

This festive scene of a marriage feast by the Flemish painter Joris Hoefnagel (c. 1569) illustrates a panorama of Elizabethan society.

Epilogue

Elizabeth died shortly before 3 a.m. on March 24, 1603. Whether she finally acknowledged James VI of Scotland as her rightful successor will never be known for certain. Since, however, James was the legitimate candidate by descent, and was male, Protestant, and available, he was supported by the nobility and Privy Council, and was proclaimed King James I of England (and Ireland) immediately. His accession brought about the dynastic union of the crowns of England and Scotland, and an end to the threat to England's security from within the British Isles.

Elizabeth's main achievements were to avert religious civil war and maintain England's integrity as an independent state in Europe after the break with Rome. Independence was guaranteed by the peace treaty that finally ended the war with Spain in 1604. With the return of peace, and the arrival in the Church of England of a new generation of university-trained Protestant ministers, the Church was able to transcend the barriers that had hitherto restricted its popularity. The Elizabethan religious settlement was confirmed at the Hampton Court Conference (January 1604). Thereafter, the Prayer Book increasingly took hold on the hearts and minds of the majority of the people, to the point where, by the 1620s, a culture of "conformity" was one of the defining features of English national identity.

As to the problems of government, Elizabeth was successful as a ruler until her regime started to buckle under the pressure of war. A woman was not best equipped to project her image as a military leader in the sixteenth century, even if Elizabeth is renowned for her speech to her troops at Tilbury in 1588. "I may have the body of a weak and feeble woman, but I have the heart and stomach of a king," she is alleged to have pronounced. Whether she actually spoke these words, or whether her speech was redrafted retrospectively by spin doctors, is open to question. The myth of Gloriana enveloped her image in the later years of her reign, and fact and fiction become blurred.

When James I pursued a policy of equivocation in foreign policy and the Thirty Years War erupted across Europe after 1618, Elizabeth was "reinvented" by the king's parliamentary critics as a decisive ruler with an unswerving commitment to the Protestant cause abroad. This was the stuff of legend. It is easy to romanticize or eulogize such Tudor triumphs as the refoundation of the monarchy, economic expansion, the Reformation, the repulse of Spain, the defeat of puritan and Catholic extremism, and the unification of Britain—finally attained on the queen's death. But reality is more abrasive. Elizabeth was a strong ruler with a winning, but often imperious, manner. She took a high view of her royal prerogative, and held as robust a belief in the divine right of kings as her father and successor. She had a sharp tongue and a smoldering temper. She could be vain, indecisive, and isolationist. Raleigh said of her foreign policy, "Her Majesty did all by halves." By the 1620s, England was unable to fight a protracted war without engendering domestic political friction. In particular, the decline in the system of taxation in the later years of Elizabeth made it harder for her successors to govern England. When civil war broke out in 1642, a contributory cause was the Crown's inability to levy sufficient taxation to meet the costs of government and diplomacy. When Clarendon later began his *History of the Rebellion and Civil Wars* he wrote: "I am not so sharpsighted as those, who have discerned this rebellion contriving from (if not before) the death of Queen Elizabeth." He knew that if we read history backwards, Elizabeth's inertia and immobility in the 1590s, combined with the problems of Ireland and of the rise of venality at court, could be said to have established a pattern that precluded comprehensive reform. The conundrum was clearly debated in Clarendon's own lifetime. History is properly read forwards, and the issue of the "success" or "failure" of Elizabethan government was overtaken during the Personal Rule of Charles I by the more significant (perceived) threat to Protestantism and the constitution of the Three Kingdoms of England, Scotland, and Ireland that was represented by the policies of the king and Archbishop Laud. Yet the late Elizabethan legacy of meager public revenue and governmental malaise was ultimately reversed only by the events of the Civil War and Interregnum.

FURTHER READING

•

GENERAL WORKS

S. G. Ellis, *Tudor Ireland: Crown, Community and the Conflict of Cultures, 1470–1603* (London, 1985), the standard textbook on Ireland.

G. R. Elton, *Reform and Reformation: England, 1509–1558* (London, 1977), the liveliest summary of Elton's mature views.

J. Guy, *Tudor England* (Oxford, 1990), a comprehensive standard textbook on the period.

C. Haigh, *English Reformations: Religion, Politics, and Society under the Tudors* (Oxford, 1993), the leading current textbook on the Reformation.

D. M. Palliser, *The Age of Elizabeth: England under the Later Tudors, 1547–1603* (London, 1983), still the best synthesis of social and economic conditions.

P. Williams, *The Tudor Regime* (Oxford, 1979), a valuable textbook focused more on social power and government in the counties than on the politics of the court and Parliament.

P. Williams, *The Later Tudors: England, 1547–1603* (Oxford, 1995), a comprehensive general survey.

J. Wormald, *Court, Kirk and Community: Scotland, 1470–1625* (London, 1981), still the best survey of sixteenth-century Scotland.

BIOGRAPHIES

S. B. Chrimes, *Henry VII* (London, 1972), a sound study, especially strong on the institutions of government.

J. Guy, *Thomas More* (London, 2000), a concise life which looks mainly at the debates over More's career and the gap between legend and fact.

P. Gwyn, *The King's Cardinal: The Rise and Fall of Thomas Wolsey* (London, 1990), a valuable summary of the latest academic research, but at wearisome length.

C. Haigh, *Elizabeth I* (Harlow, 1988), a trenchant, revisionist interpretation of the queen.

E. W. Ives, *Anne Boleyn* (Oxford, 1986), not merely a life of Anne, but the liveliest introduction to the politics of Henry VIII's reign.

J. Loach, *Edward VI* (London, 1999), an important study which illuminates a period often neglected by specialists.

D. M. Loades, *Mary Tudor: A Life* (Oxford, 1989), the most recent scholarly biography.

W. T. MacCaffrey, *Elizabeth I* (London, 1993), the most impressive scholarly biography.

D. MacCulloch, *Thomas Cranmer: A Life* (London, 1996), the outstanding biography which illuminates Cranmer's mind-set and relations with Henry VIII.

R. Marius, *Thomas More* (New York, 1984), a critical and controversial, but not unsympathetic biography.

J. E. Neale, *Queen Elizabeth I* (London, 1933), still the most accessible scholarly life of Elizabeth, but the author's opinions are dated.

M. Perry, *The Word of a Prince: A Life of Elizabeth I* (Woodbridge, 1990), a life from contemporary documents, clearly written and accessible to general readers.

J. J. Scarisbrick, *Henry VIII* (London, 1968), the classic biography, as fresh as ever despite the advances of research.

STUDIES OF SPECIAL TOPICS

S. Alford, *The Early Elizabethan Polity: William Cecil and the British Succession Crisis, 1558–1569* (Cambridge, 1998), a reassessment of the relationship of Elizabeth and Cecil.

S. Anglo, *Spectacle, Pageantry, and Early Tudor Policy* (Oxford, 1969), the fullest account of the early-Tudor court festivals and entertainments.

C. Carpenter, *The Wars of the Roses: Politics and the Constitution in England, c.1437–1509* (Cambridge, 1997), a challenging political survey, which throws down the gauntlet to traditional accounts of the reign of Henry VII.

P. Collinson, *The Elizabethan Puritan Movement* (London, 1967), a virtuoso study by the acknowledged expert.

S. Doran, *Monarchy and Matrimony: The Courtships of Elizabeth I* (London, 1996), an analytical account of Elizabeth's courtships and matrimonial diplomacy.

E. Duffy, *The Stripping of the Altars: Traditional Religion in England, 1400–1580* (London, 1992), the fullest account of the Catholic liturgical tradition on the eve of the Reformation, and a skeptical reassessment of the reaction of the people to the break with Rome.

S. G. Ellis, *Tudor Frontiers and Noble Power: The Making of the British State* (Oxford, 1995), a comparative study of the problems of government and state formation in Ireland and the borderland regions of Cumbria.

S. G. Ellis and S. Barber (eds), *Conquest and Union: Fashioning a British State, 1485–1725* (London, 1995), an essential collection of academic studies.

G. R. Elton, *Policy and Police: The Enforcement of the Reformation in the Age of Thomas Cromwell* (Cambridge, 1972), the authoritative study of Cromwell's role in the break with Rome.

S. Frye, *Elizabeth I: The Competition for Representation* (New York, 1993), a feminist study of ways in which Elizabeth's power was constructed in a male-dominated society.

J. Guy (ed.), *The Reign of Elizabeth I: Court and Culture in the Last Decade* (Cambridge, 1995), a useful collection of essays on the later years of the reign.

J. Guy (ed.), *The Tudor Monarchy* (London, 1997), a collection of important essays by leading historians on politics and the monarchy.

H. Hackett, *Virgin Mother, Maiden Queen: Elizabeth I and the Cult of the Virgin Mary* (New York, 1995), an academic study of the legends that circumscribe Elizabeth from the perspective of gender.

C. Levin, *The Heart and Stomach of a King: Elizabeth I and the Politics of Sex and Power* (Philadelphia, 1994), a feminist reassessment which seeks to understand the role of gender in the exercise of power.

J. Loach and R. Tittler (eds), *The Mid-Tudor Polity* (London, 1980), a valuable antidote to the old-fashioned platitudes about the 1550s.

W. T. MacCaffrey, *The Shaping of the Elizabethan Regime: Elizabethan Politics, 1558–72* (London, 1969), the first volume of an academic trilogy on the reign.

W. T. MacCaffrey, *Queen Elizabeth and the Making of Policy, 1572–1588* (Princeton, 1981), the second volume of the trilogy, which is especially good on the Netherlands and the Anjou marriage negotiations.

W. T. MacCaffrey, *Elizabeth I: War and Politics, 1588–1603* (Princeton, 1992), the final volume of the trilogy, which covers the European war and revolt in Ireland.

D. MacCulloch (ed.), *The Reign of Henry VIII: Politics, Policy and Piety* (London, 1995), valuable essays aimed at history students.

R. Rex, *Henry VIII and the English Reformation* (London, 1993), a brief and helpful summary for students.

D. R. Starkey, *The Reign of Henry VIII: Personalities and Politics* (London, 1985), a lively account of court politics and faction.

R. Strong, *The Cult of Elizabeth: Elizabethan Portraiture and Pageantry* (London, 1977), a general introduction to Elizabethan iconography.

WEB SITES

Institute of Historical Research, University of London: **www.ihr.sas.ac.uk**

Author: **www.tudors.org**

CHRONOLOGY

•

1542	Battle of Solway Moss; English victory over invading Scottish army
1543	War with France: English capture of Boulogne
1547	Succession of Edward VI; ascendancy of Protector Somerset; battle of Pinkie: English victory over Scotland
1549	First Book of Common Prayer; Warwick's coup
1553	Accession of Mary
1554	Wyatt's rebellion; Pole returns; reunion with Rome
1555	Persecution of Protestants begins
1557	War with France
1558	New Book of Rates; accession of Elizabeth I
1559	Peace of Cateau-Cambrésis; religious Settlement in England
1566	Archbishop Parker's *Advertisements* demand religious conformity
1568	Mary Stuart flees to England
1569	Northern Rising
1570	Papal bull declares Elizabeth excommunicated and deposed
1580	Jesuit missionaries arrive in England
1585	Leicester's intervention in the Netherlands; war with Spain
1587	Execution of Mary Stuart
1588	Defeat of the Spanish Armada
1594	Bad harvests begin
1601	Essex's rebellion
1603	Death of Elizabeth; accession of James VI of Scotland as James I; peace in Ireland

Genealogical Tree

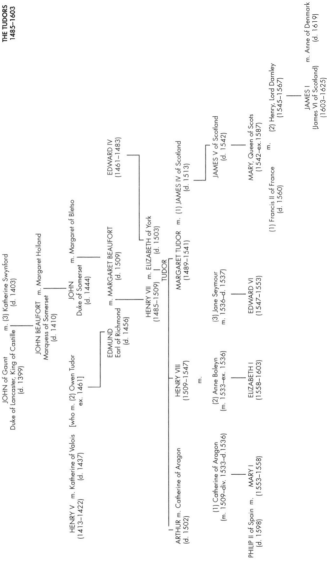

INDEX

•

Page numbers in *italics* include illustrations and photographs/captions.

PICTURE CREDITS

•

London, UK / The Bridgeman Art Library

Hertfordshire; 99: Cecil Court of Wards; 105: Robert Dudley Graaf van Leicester Rijksmuseum Ravesteyn / Rijksmuseum Amsterdam; 108: Francois Second Mary Stuart; 110: Debat-Ponsan-matin-Louvre; 113: Vertooninge van de ontsachlyke Spaansche krygs vloot, in den jaare 1588 - The mighty display of the Spanish armada in 1588 (Jan Luyken) / Amsterdams Historisch Museum; 117: Elizabeth I in Parliament; 124: Hardwick Hall 4 / Phil Sangwell; 132: 1623 Shakespeare Folio-edition-p-xvii / Uploaded by Olaf Simons; 134: Joris Hoefnagel Fete at Bermondsey c 1569 / Private Collection

BRIEF INSIGHTS

•

A series of concise, engrossing, and enlightening books that explore
every subject under the sun with unique insight.

Available now or coming soon: